LORD OF THE SMOKIES

An Appalachian Folk Play

by

Myla Lichtman-Fields

Myla Productions
MylaProds@aol.com
website: mylalichtmanfields.com

Member Dramatists Guild of America

ISBN 978-1-329-11515-6

Dedicated to the memory of **BORIS APLON**, a marvelous Broadway performer and the first Uncle Homer in the musical version of LORD OF THE SMOKIES (aka THADIUS STEED) at USC.

and

Dedicated to the memory of Norris Theater Artistic Director **MICHAEL PUTNAM** who played Thadius Steed in the Norris Theater's New Play Discovery series' presentation of LORD OF THE SMOKIES.

and

Dedicated to the memory of **AGNES MOSS** who was my "angel" at The Norris Theater. She arranged for my seat on the Management Board, for my Executive Producer position of the theater's Opening Festival, for my UCLA Dramatic Writing classes at the theater, and for the backing for The Norris Theater's New Play Discovery Series, which I produced over a period of 3 years, and in which LORD OF THE SMOKIES was the first offering.

CAST OF CHARACTERS
(In the order in which they speak)

UNCLE HOMER STEED, Thadius Steed's uncle, nearly blind story-teller.

THADIUS STEED, moonshiner, protector of the community, grizzly-bear-of-a-man.

LEM OWNBY, mountain man married to Hettie.

THISBE OGLE, mountain man married to Arbyzena.

FATE O'DARE, young daughter of Manuel and Polly, betrothed to Thadius.

MANUEL O'DARE, husband of Polly and father of Fate, farmer.

POLLY O'DARE, wife of Manuel and mother of Fate.

ARBYZENA OGLE, area gossip, wife and mother.

GRANNY LOUZILTHY SETTER, old flame of Uncle Homer, eldest female in community.

HETTIE OWNBY, wife of Lem and mother of Ebeneezer.

EBENEEZER OWNBY, in his teens.

ARMINTA OGLE, Arbyzena's daughter, a heavyset teen.

HYRAM STEED, medical doctor, younger brother of Thadius.

REVEREND FOBIDIAH WENTWORTH, *little parson of the hills* since childhood.

ORVAL SPEAR, Virginia coal miner.

NANCY SPEAR, Orval's wife.

MONTAINFOLK, CHILDREN, and MINERS

NOTE: Double-casting is feasible and **can enable a smaller cast** to perform this work.

There should be consistency in pronunciations by the mountainfolk within the play. **Words that are affected are:** *you*=yew; **your=yer; all** *ing* endings should be pronounced **minus the final** *g*; and **for=fer.** HYRAM and the LITTLE PARSON and the mining community will not use these mountain pronunciations.

SYNOPSIS OF SCENES
PROLOGUE

Steed's Holler at the base of Thunder Gap in the southern Appalachian mountains.

Early morning in May of 1910.

ACT ONE: SUMMER

Scene 1:   Fate's mountain bald.
                  Same time as prologue.

Scene 2:   Cabin of the O'Dares.
                  Later that same morning.

Scene 3:   Steed's homestead.
                  Later that same morning.

Scene 4:   Bedroom of Thadius Steed.
                  Night of the same day.

Scene 5:   Steed's homestead.
                  Early morning of the next day.

ACT TWO: AUTUMN

Scene 1:   Inside a coal mine in
                  Virginia.
                  November of 1910.

Scene 2:   Fate's mountain bald.
                  Sunrise of the same day.

Scene 3: Steed's homestead.
Same day as previous
scene.

Scene 4: The Spear's shack in
Virginia.
Evening of the next day.

Scene 5: Steed's homestead.
Night of the following day.

ACT THREE: WINTER

Scene 1: Steed's homestead.
January of 1911.

Scene 2: Fate's mountain bald.
Later that same night.

Scene 3: Steed's homestead.
The following morning.

EPILOGUE

Fate's mountain bald.
Sunrise of the following
day.

NOTE: "LORD OF THE SMOKIES" was
performed as a 2-Act play when the play was
presented as a staged reading at The Norris Theatre.
The **INTERMISSION** occurred **between Act
Two and Act Three.**

SETTING

Steed's Holler at the base of Thunder Gap
in the heart of the Smoky Mountains,
Tennessee. Circa 1910.

A cleared pioneer settlement centered
around a towering hemlock tree, beneath
which traveling preachers come to
sermonize, weddings are held, and
community gatherings occur.

On a side stage Stage-Right (S.R.),protruding
partially onto the stage and on a level slightly
above that of the stage floor, is the porch of the
Steed Home--a hewn log cabin. UNCLE
HOMER STEED's rocker is located on the
porch atop the three uneven porch steps.

Left of Center-Stage (C.S.) is a tree stump
which will serve as lectern for visiting
preachers and as a congregating spot for
community festivities.

Slightly upstage and Stage-Left (S.L.) is a
large boulder containing many step-like
levels along its rounded ascent towards the
summit of the S.L. side stage. This side stage
S.L. represents FATE O'DARE's mountain
bald--a meadow atop a lushly wooded
mountain overlooking Steed's Holler and the
surrounding cove settlement below. This
should be the highest playing area.

A cyclorama encircles the entire stage playing area and is located upstage. Painted cut-out trees of the lushly wooded Smoky Mountains are stylistically highlighted against a stark white background through which colors of the seasons and times of day within the play will be reflected.

BEFORE THE CURTAIN:MUSIC, an orchestra--of banjo, harmonica, dulcimer, and guitar--gradually winds the audience's expectancy into a wild frenetic foot-stomping pace. Then, one instrument at a time drops out of the fray leaving only the amplified sound of the whirling Appalachian Hornet--a stringed instrument whirled to create the sound of a hornet's frenzy--to set off the PROLOGUE.

NOTE: This production can be entirely staged utilizing the **singular setting** described. Set decoration can serve to represent the various homesteads. Minimal settings can be used to convey the coal mine and Virginia sequences. The primary set described can be used exclusively for the major portion of the play.

GLOSSARY OF MOUNTAIN TERMS

1. **furriner (or outlander)** -- Someone who comes from the area outside the Smoky Mountains.

2. **highlander** -- A native of the Smoky Mountain community.

3. **Revenuer** -- A most unwelcome "*furrine*r". A Probation Officer who works for the U.S. Department of Internal Revenue whose job it is to crack down on the producers of illegal moonshine whiskey.

4. **Devil's Brew** -- Mountain term for moonshine corn whiskey.

5. **gap** -- A gap is located at the point where two mountains come together Those less fortunate settlers live in these areas.

6. **holler** -- A holler is a cove at the base of a gap. It is usually flat and desirable for building homes and for farming.

7. **hant** -- A ghost.

8. **bar** -- Mountain pronunciation of the word "*bear*".

9. **Appalachian** -- The mountains whose southern ranges contain the Smokies.
Pronounced "*Appalatchian*".

PROLOGUE

Only the Hemlock tree is lit.
It is early morning of June, 1910. A
RIFLE SHOT RINGS OUT. MUSIC, an
orchestra of banjo, harmonica, and
guitar, gradually wind the audience's
expectancy into a wild frenetic foot-
stomping pace. Then, one instrument at
a time drops out of the fray, leaving only
the sound of the whirring Appalachian
Hornet--a stringed instrument whirled to
create the sound of a hornet's frenzy--as
the LIGHTS BEGIN COMING UP on
UNCLE HOMER'S PORCH ROCKER.
A SECOND RIFLE SHOT RINGS OUT.
HOMER'S ROCKER builds its
momentum, as the ninety-year-old
mountain man chomps his "Blood
Hound" chewing tobacco and anxiously
rocks on the front porch of his hand
hewn mountain cabin.
A THIRD RIFLE SHOT RINGS OUT,
followed by the pained wail of a
WOUNDED BEAR in the distance.
Homer's HUNTING DOG, Wheezer, tied
to a rope underneath the house, BAYS
WILDLY.
HOMER, knowing what has happened in
the woods, sits bolt upright in his chair.
He inhales and releases a bullet-like
chug of TOBACCO, which STRIKES the

old BRASS SHIP'S BELL on the porch
overhang. (The bell, brought over from
Ireland, reads "MCTAVISH-STEED 1800".)
The BELL CLANGS. HOMER SLAPS his
wirey old KNEES and HOOTS LIKE A
BEAR.

HOMER: Wooooooooweeeeeeeeee! Meanest devil's
gonna win out. Sounds like Thadius has got hisself
another killin'. Sure as this be a *shivaree* day!

(Upstage BRANCHES PART. THADIUS STEED, a
grizzley-faced man, giant-like in his overalls barrels
towards C.S. He RAISES HIS RIFLE to his eye and
takes aim--at the audience. SHOOTS.
A PROLONGED WAIL issues forth from the twice-
wounded BLACK BEAR. THADIUS GRINS,
seething with the taste of victory. He emits a wild
bear-like grunt:)

THADIUS: Raaaaaaaaaaaaaaaaaaaah!

(HOMER is standing at the porch railing, listening.
Because of his cataracts, HOMER is unable to see
the BEAR in the distance. The UPSTAGE
BRANCHES PART, as THISBE and LEM--poker-
faced mountain men--come upon THADIUS, who
motions for them to stay back. THADIUS is
sighting the bear through his rifle rangefinder. THE
BEAR IS WAILING IN PAIN.)

HOMER: Finish him off, Thadius. Finish him off!

12

(Resolved, THADIUS lowers his rifle, as THE BEAR'S WAILS continue. THADIUS stares at his victim, victoriously:)

THADIUS: Nope. He's gotta seethe and stew 'til his brains boil with hatred. Then when my new bride gal tastes just one bite of his ornery meat, she'll more 'n certain bar me a son as full of savagery as that black demon thar.

 (The BEAR'S PAINED MOANS are UNDERSCORED by the HORNET'S WHIR, which grows in VOLUME.)

HOMER: There's more kinds of hellfire than jest killin' for the heck of it, Nephew.
(Looking out towards the BEAR) No critter's pain oughta give us that much pleasure. (Anger mounting, to THADIUS) Finish him off, now! Finish him off!

THISBE: (Pleading) Please, Thadius?

LEM: Ya gotta!

THADIUS: Gotta! Hell's afire!

THISBE: Uncle Homer's right, Thad.

THADIUS: Go suck your bottle, Thisbe.

LEM: It's devil's play.

THADIUS: *Devil*. Hell!

(Riled, THADIUS RAISES THE RIFLE and SLAYS THE BEAR.

The animal's FINAL WAIL LASTS FOR SEVERAL UNNATURAL BEATS. Then the body is HEARD DROPPING to the GROUND.
UNCLE HOMER FLOPS DOWN into his ROCKER, wiping his forehead with his kerchief:)

HOMER: (Relieved) Merciful Lord.

(THADIUS MOUNTS THE TREE STUMP downstage left:)

THADIUS: (Triumphant wail towards the heavens)
You're in me now Lord! (To THISBE and LEM, who have begun to move towards the BEAR) Leave him be! No man crosses paths with Thadius steed, 'less they be fixin' for a bout with the Devil hisself. Hear me?

LEM: We hear ya, Thadius.

THISBE: You're the protector of this community. Ain't no denyin' it, Thad.

THISBE: Don't you want us to be skinnin' it for ya?

(THADIUS steps down from the stump and begins to head towards the porch steps. He calls back over his shoulder:)

THADIUS: Yup. I gotta be gettin' myself ready for the big hoopla. (Slapping UNCLE HOMER'S shoulders) Ain't that right, Uncle?

HOMER: Today's the *big day* all right.

(THADIUS EXITS into the cabin. HOMER EXITS, following after him. LEM and THISBE are SHARPENING THEIR KNIVES on STONES, preparing to skin the bear.)

LEM: Ain't none meaner.

THISBE: Cold blooded.

LEM: He'll get his comeuppance.

THISBE: Had two wives die on him. Think he'd be scared of takin' hisself another.

LEM: *Scared*? Thadius? (Holding the KNIFE UP) Lucifer!

THISBE: Granny Setter says there's a curse on him since he shot up them Revenuers.

LEM: (Looking towards cabin door) Notice he's been placin' witch hobble leaves above his doorway.

THISBE: No male heir. One thing he wants real bad.

LEM: Right now he wants that bear skinned.

(LEM and THISBE EXIT to skin the bear.

UNCLE HOMER EXITS THE HOUSE, carrying a
METAL WATERPAIL. HOMER goes to the PUMP.
FILLS THE PAIL. PAUSES for a moment to look
out towards the BEAR.)

THADIUS OFF-STAGE: (Shouting)
Raaaaaaaaaaaaaaaaaaaaah!

HOMER: (Sadly, to the AUDIENCE) Warriors.
All get their skinning times. Sure as the sun makes
us sweat when we get to actin' too ornery.
(SPITS A TOBACCO PLUG, striking the PORCH
BELL) So, now it's begun. Be takin' hisself a third
wife today. Innocent flower, nigh half his age. Lord
only knows what'll happen once he unleashes his
wildness on her. Poor Fate O'Dare.

(BLACK OUT.)

END OF PROLOGUE.

ACT ONE
SCENE ONE

In the BLACK OUT the
sound of a rushing STREAM IS HEARD.
A COW BELL is HEARD RINGING.
The LIGHTS COME UP on FATE
O'DARE, a mountain girl in her teens,
barefooted and wearing a smock dress.
She is standing atop her mountain bald
elevated playing area S.L. looking down
the hillside towards LUCY, her father's
prize milk cow.

FATE: (Calling) Lucy! No use hidin'. I see you down there, you old milch cow. We'll both belong to Thadius Steed come sunset....Like it or not. It's agreed.

(FATE flops down upon the ground, continuing to look down at the mountain world sprawling all around her.)

FATE: (Continuing, Touching her breast, thoughtfully) Why does it have to change? Spring breathed her life into me just like it done to our pear tree. Now's the time I gotta be picked, and begin puttin' down some roots of my own....But, I'm scared. . . .

17

(OFF-STAGE VOICE OF POLLY O'DARE--
FATE'S mother--is HEARD coming from the base of
the mountain:)

POLLY OFF-STAGE: (Calling) Daughter! Fate
O'Dare!

FATE: (Snapped from her reverie, calls down the
hill) Comin' Ma. Comin'! (Calling towards the
COW) Gotta get you home, Lucy. It'll be the last
time we can call it that. So let's get.

(FATE begins descending the mountain. STOPS.
Once again reflecting:)

FATE: (Continuing) Granny Setter, I know what
you'd say to me now. *'Ain't never gonna be no
fairytale prince to come take you away to heaven,
girl!'* I know I oughta be a thankin' the good Lord for
the man my Pa's done picked for me. Someone
who'll need me. Someone I guess I can learn to love
with time. (Looking down towards THADIUS
STEED'S HOMESTEAD) They'll be gatherin'
round the marryin' tree, soon now. (Examining her
body with her hand) I'm just bursting with
wondering how it'll be, 'n all.... (Anxiously, almost
prayerfully) Thadius Steed, please,...please be
gentle with me.

(BLACK OUT. The RUSHING STREAM
UNDERSCORES during the black out.)

SCENE TWO
*The LIGHTS COME UP
on the modest dining table of the
O'DARE cabin. The stern-faced
MANUEL O'DARE is seated at the
breakfast table. He eats in
SILENCE. POLLY is serving MANUEL a
basket of freshly baked bread. He tears
the bread roll and dips it into his coffee.
FATE ENTERS, drying her face and
hands on her skirt:*

FATE: Pump's actin' up again. Squirted me good.

MANUEL: (Sternly) Sit yourself down, Daughter.

(The O'DARE CABIN contains a LARGE DOUBLE
BRASS BED covered by a colorful quilt. A LARGE
TIN-TYPE FRAMED PHOTO of MANUEL'S
FATHER in A UNION ARMY UNIFORM, bearing
the same cold stare as his offspring, hangs above the
bed. FATE's bed is in another corner of the one-
room cabin. It is made of straw and is covered with
quilts. There are wildflowers pressed and pinned to
the walls around her bed, along with treasured
cards, a braided yarn doll, an apple doll, and a
DULCIMER (stringed instrument) hung from a wall
peg. A FIRE BLAZES in the hearth in the other
corner of the room. A large mush kettle hangs over
the hearth and POLLY stirs it and ladles out a bowl
full for FATE:)

POLLY: Here y'are, Daughter.

FATE: (Taking the food to the table)
Thanks, Ma. I'm gonna take my time eatin' it.
(To MANUEL) Mama's weddin' dress looks real
purty on me, Pa.   Just wait'll you see it.

POLLY: Like seein' myself at your age, Daughter.

(POLLY shoots MANUEL a pleading look, which he
rebuffs, averting her eyes. He hands her his bowl,
which she mechanically takes and refills

FATE: I was hopin' that this bein' my weddin' day 'n
all, you two might start talkin' to each other,...try
mendin' your--

MANUEL: Fetch me the cream, Daughter.

FATE: Yes, Pa. (Getting the pitcher from the
window sill) Here y' are, Pa.

MANUEL: And, tell your Ma we best be leavin'
round eleven.

FATE: (To POLLY) Pa said we'd best be leavin' at
eleven.

POLLY: (Upset) Tell your Pa I ain't about to be late
to my own daughter's weddin'.

 (MANUEL is finished eating. He EXITS the cabin
before FATE has finished relaying the message to
him:)

FATE: Ma says she ain't about to be late to her own daughter's weddin', Pa--

POLLY: He knows....Stubborn mule!

FATE: (Concerned) What'll you do, Ma? With me gone?

POLLY: (Clearing the table) Expect the silence'll kill me. Hard enough with you here. But without ya--

(POLLY breaks down, covering her face with her apron. FATE moves to her mother's side, helping POLLY to sit in one of the split-bottomed chairs:)

FATE: (Soothingly) It just can't go on, Ma.

POLLY: (Dabbing her eyes) Just remember, Daughter. Once you're a man's woman, you gotta stand by him, whether he's right or hell-brained wrong. You gotta love him, no matter what. 'Cause you're his.

FATE: But, Ma, it ain't right for one person to own another.

POLLY: *Own?* A marriage contract's bindin' in the eyes of the Lord. Don't you never forget that.

FATE: But, I don't even know Thadius Steed. Never spoke more 'n a few words to him. I'm so scared.

POLLY: His is the best homestead round these parts. And he'll make you his Queen of Cataloochee Cove.

FATE: But, what'll we talk about?

POLLY: *Talk*!...Talkin' ain't the only thing, girl. It's what you do that matters. The little things.

(FATE and POLLY are removing candles from the candle rack where they have finished drying. They place the candles in a small wooden box.)

FATE: Like candle makin'?

POLLY: Washin' and cookin', too. Yup....
 (Looking towards the BED she shares with MANUEL) Or, just lyin' side-by-side together in the night.

 (POLLY begins combing FATE's hair.)

FATE: Pa don't treat you right, he--

POLLY: I done wrong. I'm payin' for my sin. Payin' for it ' til I die, I expect. My Cross.

FATE: (Reacting to painful hair-tangle)
Ouuuuuuuch!

POLLY: Stand still! Can't pretty you up if'n you
keep movin' like a chicken with its head off.

FATE: (Imitating a rooster crowing)
Cockadoodle--doo!

 (FATE and POLLY BREAK INTO LAUGHTER.
POLLY's nervousness leads to tears.
FATE holds POLLY, comforting her:)

FATE: (Continuing, Soothingly)
Oh, Mama!

 (BLACK OUT.)

SCENE THREE

*The inhabitants of Cataloochee Cove are
arriving at Steed's Holler. They are carrying
cakes, fiddles, dulcimers, jugs of moonshine
whiskey, and other items that will
contribute to the wedding celebration.
GRANNY SETTER is toting a large quilt for
the newlyweds. The men start tuning up their
fiddles and playing a foot-stomping tune, as
ARBYZENA OGLE--the community gossip--
arrives with her high-strung husband, THISBE,
and her heavyset daughter, ARMINTA.*

ARBYZENA: (Scolding) Hold your head up, Arminta! Never land yourself a man if you keep walking with your snout to the mud.

(GRANNY SETTER is seated on HOMER's porch beside the old man. Together, they are observing the preparations.)

GRANNY: (Confidentially, to HOMER) Landsakes, but that Arbyzena's gonna make a wall flower out of that daughter of hers yet. Or, drive her to Lord knows what!

HOMER: People bring miseries on themselves. (Calling to THISBE) Bring a fresh brew with ya, Thisbe?

(ARBYZENA and ARMINTA have joined HETTIE OWNBY setting up a buffet table of after-wedding delicacies: funnel cakes, preserves, pickled pigs snouts and feet, and assorted pies. THISBE has seated himself upon the porch steps near HOMER. The **CONVERSATION at the BUFFET TABLE OVERLAPS the CONVERSATION on the PORCH**.)

THISBE: (Holding whiskey jug up) Best moonshine this side of the Blue Ridge.

ARBYZENA: (To HETTIE) Callie Kear's expectin' again.

24

HOMER: Put it right here near me, son. Just havin' it near me makes my blood rise.

HETTIE: (Clicking her tongue) No telling who the father is. She's no better than that wild sister of hers we buried over on the far side of the cemetery.

ARBYZENA: Away from our good Christian folk.

GRANNY: (Chuckling, to HOMER)
Sure that's what's makin' your blood rise, you old fox?

HOMER: (Patting GRANNY's hand)
Louzilthy, you just stay set right where you are. The sunshine don't find its way to this porch ever too often.

(GRANNY smiles, pleased.)

GRANNY: You do have a way with words, Homer Steed.

(ARBYZENA slaps ARMINTA's hand as the heavyset teen reaches for a piece of funnel cake.)

ARBYZENA: Arminta! Hold your horses, girl. There'll be plenty of eatin' *after* the weddin' .
(Taking her aside) And don't you be givin' Thadius the eye. He's took. You be 'aworkin' on that younger brother of his when he gets here.

(THE FIDDLERS are playing up a storm and are joined by young EBENEEZER OWNBY, who plays banjo. ARBYZENA exchanges knowing glaces with HETTIE OWNBY before speaking to ARMINTA:)

ARBYZENA: (Continuing) Oh, get yourself away from here, Daughter. We can take care of the fixins.

(ARMINTA wanders over to the musicians. She stands, leaning against the hemlock tree, fanning herself coquettishly with a straw fan, in rhythm to the music.)

HETTIE: (Calling across the stage, to GRANNY) Granny, did you bring the marryin' rope?

GRANNY: (Holding the rope up, to HETTIE) Here 'tis. Same one I brung to your weddin' day, Hettie Ownby. (Rising from her rocker, to HOMER) Guess I best be gettin' over there to help with that spread. (Winking, devilishly)
Don't want to be missin' out on nothing.

(GRANNY goes over to the buffet table.)

HOMER: (To THISBE, who 's seated on the porch steps) We don't need any of them newfangled tel-ee-phones round here. Something happens, it's wildfire. Women's tongues. Menfolk's glances. (Amused, confidentially) Thadius is in there primpin' like a woman. Hair oil. Socks changed. Even used the comb!

THISBE: Didn't think Thadius owned none.

HOMER: I give it to him. Besides, deep down under he's the same as all us menfolk.

THISBE: Better at hell-raising than any I knowed.

HOMER: Black bar, for sure. But, we got his organizin' ways to thank for our mountain patrol.

THISBE: We's all obliged to him. These mountains are everything to Thadius.

HOMER: Community's safer cause of Thadius. No doubt about it. Jest remember, he ain't all black bar. Sure, he's playin' his part real good, takin' care of us all. But, deep down underneath, he's needin' to be pampered just like a youngun.

THISBE: Seems to me, any man who had hisself two wives, who both up and died on him, would be scared of takin' on another.

HOMER: (Ominously) Oh, he's worryin'. He'd die before he'd ever admit his feelings to hisself. That's his problem. Thadius thinks feelings is just for womenfolk--

(HOMER is interrupted by the ENTRANCE of THADIUS, who ENTERS the porch from the cabin. THADIUS' tall muscular hulk is giant-like. The MUSIC STOPS as ALL STARE at the community leader and groom-to-be.
LEM calls out to THADIUS from across the yard:)

LEM: Woooooooooweeeeeeee! Thadius, don't you look fit to kill!

THADIUS: (Stretching his arms, bear-like growl) Rrrrrrrrrrrraaaaaaaaaaah! (To THISBE) That Parson get here yet?

THISBE: Uriah sent word the little fella's on his way.

THADIUS: (Wandering over to the MUSICIANS) Keep the music a goin' boys. Wanna raise a hell of a ruckus so's all heaven'll hear Thadius Steed's takin' hisself a male-heir-bearing bride this day!

(The WOMEN'S tongues cluck at THADIUS' irreverent audacity. The MUSICIANS RESUME THEIR PLAYING.)

ARMINTA: Thadius has got hisself one *mean* tongue.

(THADIUS strides over to the buffet table. He PLUNGES HIS FINGERS INTO AN OPEN JAR OF SOURWOOD HONEY. Then, licks the dripping goo:)

THADIUS: Sweet Jesus!

(THADIUS smacks his lips. The WOMEN CHIME IN, echoing their approval:)

WOMEN: Amen.

28

GRANNY: Sweet as *honey*, indeed!

HETTIE: (Proudly) That honey's from our sourwood stand over by our cow shed, Thadius. Brung it special for your weddin' day.

THADIUS: (Kissing HETTIE) And I won't forget it, neither.

(HETTIE blushes. ARBYZENA is eyeing ARMINTA, who's across the yard near the musicians.)

ARMINTA: Heard word from that brother of yours, Thadius?

THADIUS: Hyram sent word he's comin' home for the weddin'. Should've been here by now. (Proudly) Not all Steeds are lead-headed. Got hisself top marks at that medical college. Now we gotta be calling him '*Doctor* Hyram Steed'!

GRANNY: He's got you to thank, Thadius, for putting him through that fancy medical school.

ARBYZENA: (Angling on her daughter's behalf) Saw to it my Arminta learned to read *The Good Book*. Not a bad head on her shoulders, . . . for a girl.

THADIUS: (Scooping another finger-full of honey, smacking his lips) Ain't her *head* you oughta be worryin' about, Arbyzena.

(THADIUS strides over to TWO CHILDREN playing with a wooden propeller toy:)

THADIUS: (Continuing) That's quite a Geewhimmydiddle you got yourself there, Martha Whaley.

(THADIUS continues down to the water pump. ARMINTA follows after him:)

ARMINTA: Thadius, you're lookin' mighty purty.

THADIUS: It's finished between us, girlee.

ARMINTA: Ain't no *'girlee'*. Keep telling you. I'm a woman full growed.

THADIUS: So?

ARMINTA: (Seductively) Always thought you liked me, Thadius. I've had a hankerin' for so long now--

THADIUS: (Stopping her) I'm getting married today, girl. Ain't you got no pride?

ARMINTA: No. Not too proud to speak my feelings. You're a grizzly bar for certain. I'm the only one around here can give you that male heir you've been hankerin' for.

THADIUS: (Swilling water, wipes his mouth on his sleeve) Just keep your paws off my kid brother. Hear?

ARMINTA: You're makin' a big mistake, Mister Thadius Steed. You don't know which side your bread's buttered on.

THADIUS: Too much lard chokes a man.

ARMINTA: (Stung) You'll pay for your unfeeling ways. Leading me on all these past months. Promising things--

THADIUS: (Grabbing her hands) Slut! Every man says things in the dark.

LEM: (Calling) They're coming, Thadius!

(THADIUS walks away from ARMINTA, heading back towards the GROUP. THADIUS has come to LEM, who is standing on a crate, pointing off-stage:)

LEM: They're coming, Thadius. All three of 'em. And Manuel's bringing that prize milch cow of his.

EBENEEZER: Lucy's the best milch cow around. You're a mighty lucky man, Thadius.

ARMINTA: (Unable to restrain herself) Why, my Pa's got hisself a flood raisin' milch cow. Our Mattie don't never have to swat flies off no one but her own behind!

(The MEN CHUCKLE at ARMINTA's outburst, as the girl stomps back to the table where the WOMEN are working. LEM points off-stage left:)

LEM: They're rounding the top of the bald.

(THADIUS is shading his eyes in order to see them coming:)

THADIUS: Sweet flower. Ripe for the picking she is.

(The WOMEN are shading their eyes, looking out at the approaching O'DARE FAMILY--POLLY, MANUEL, and FATE.)

ARBYZENA: Whoever thought the Lord would bring such fortune to that clan. Living the way they done all these years.

HETTIE: Wonder if today's gonna break down that wall between Polly 'n Manuel.

GRANNY: Sixteen years of silence. Downright unGodly. No good can come of it.

HETTIE: Mountain grudges is one thing. Husband and wife's another.

ARMINTA: (Whispering in a gossiping tone) Did Polly really get herself in the family way by the *Bull?*

GRANNY: Sure looked to be so. 'Course we was all took by him. Mean handsome devil that no-good Revenuer. Always allowin' our menfolk to pay him off under the table.

ARBYZENA: Thadius sure took the wind out of his sails.

ARMINTA: Shot that *Bull* right through the gizzard, I heard tell.

GRANNY: Adultery's a sin before the Lord. Ain't none of us should never forget it.

ARMINTA: Wasn't Thadius' wife doing the carrying on with that Bull. Manuel O'Dare should've been the one doing the killing--

GRANNY: Guess we're all a bit guilty, letting Thadius do our dirty work for us. Maybe it was Manuel O'Dare's wife. But Manuel, he ain't the killin' type. Thadius Steed *is.*

ARBYZENA: Got us no use for Revenuers sniffing around our parts.

HETTIE: Thadius didn't take to that *Bull* fella sniffing round his whiskey still.

ARMINTA: (Concerned) But Thadius snuffed him. What about the "*Thou shalt not kill*," in the *Ten Golden Rules*?

GRANNY: That's for certain, girl. I worry plenty about Thadius. No running away from all he's done. Acts wilder than run away horses at times, protecting us by his unGodly acts. I'm 'afeared his judgment day'll come. (Concerned) I hope that Fate O'Dare will manage somehow to get 'ahold of his bridle. Wake him up before it's too late.

HETTIE: Here they come.

ARMINTA: For a bride, she don't look too happy.

GRANNY: That child weren't born into no loving home. (Calling to THADIUS) No talking to the bride before the ceremony, Thadius!

(THADIUS goes off with MANUEL O'DARE. FATE and POLLY head towards the buffet table.)

MANUEL: I put the milch cow in your lower pasture. Didn't know if you'd want her took to your milking shed.

THADIUS: Fine hunk 'o cow. Let's take her to the shed. I ain't supposed to be near the bride before the ceremony. . . .'*Papa*'.

(THADIUS bursts into LAUGHTER, slapping MANUEL's back. Both MEN EXIT together. The

WOMEN are admiring FATE's hand-me-down bridal gown:)

GRANNY: A beautiful picture for these tired eyes.

FATE: Thanks, Granny. 'Twas Mama's.

POLLY: And her grandmother's before that.

ARMINTA: (Seeing HYRAM approach) He's here! Our Hyram's come home to us!

(HYRAM STEED, Thadius' younger brother, ENTERS from S.L. He is tall and sensitive looking. Quite the opposite of Thadius.)

LEM: (Slapping HYRAM's back) Just wait 'til Thadius lays eyes on you!

HYRAM: I can't believe how good it is to be home again.

(LEM snorts, exchanging his amusement with the other MENFOLK. HYRAM walks over to the buffet table.)

ARMINTA: Don't you look *citified*, Hyram Steed!

GRANNY: (Correcting her) *Doctor* Hyram Steed.

HYRAM: *No one can heal better than Granny Louzilthy Setter.*

(HYRAM kisses GRANNY's hand.)

GRANNY: Always makin' me blush with that *poem-writin'* of yours, Hyram.

(As HYRAM straightens up, he suddenly sees FATE O'DARE. A LONG SPEECHLESS BEAT ensues as the immediate attraction between HYRAM and FATE is apparent upon their first glance of one another.)

FATE: Welcome home, Hyram.

HYRAM: This can't be Manuel O'Dare's *little* girl?

FATE: Not *little* anymore.

HYRAM: (Kissing FATE's hand) Princess of the Glen.

ARBYZENA: (Riled) Ain't proper fraternizing with the bride before the ceremony.

GRANNY: Arbyzena's right. We'd best get you inside, Fate O'Dare.

(The WOMEN EXIT into the cabin. The MENFOLK gather around HYRAM.)

LEM: That's one handsome animal you rode in on.

HYRAM: Thadius gave him to me for a graduation present .

(THADIUS ENTERS, comes to HYRAM, embracing him, warmly:)

THADIUS: Kid brother. (Looking HYRAM over) Don't you look *the dandy*!

HYRAM: You haven't changed at all, Thad.

THADIUS: Got a little meaner, maybe. So, you better stay in line. Hear?

HYRAM: I'm not a kid anymore, Thadius. I've seen death and dying.

THADIUS: You're still my *kid brother.* You'll be putting all that medical training of yours to good use here, now.

HYRAM: I'm planning to--

THADIUS: Uncle Homer, bring us that special jug of Devil's Brew.

(HOMER gets down on his hands and knees, removes a floor board from the porch and extricates the "*special*" keg of brew from its hiding place. The old man, with the aid of his twisted walking stick, comes down the porch steps with the keg.
HYRAM, who has been watching HOMER with deep affection, embraces him:)

HYRAM: I sure have missed your tall tales, Uncle Homer.

HOMER: Glad you're a doctor now, Nephew. Could use myself some of your mending ways.

(THADIUS takes a long chug from the whiskey bottle.)

THADIUS: Whhhooooooooooooooosh!   Baptism by firewater! Your turn, kid brother.

(HYRAM takes the bottle:)

HYRAM: (Toasting) Devil have his due!

(HYRAM takes a swallow and immediately begins choking. THADIUS chortles, slapping HYRAM's back:)

THADIUS: We gotta toughen you up, kid brother.

(HOMER is taking his turn with the whiskey bottle when GUN SHOTS RING OUT IN THE DISTANCE. THE MENFOLK FREEZE, taking note of the signal to make sure it's not Revenuers.)

THISBE: (Taking the whiskey bottle from HOMER) Ain't Revenuers.

LEM: Uriah's signaling 'cause the Little Parson's crossing into the gap. (To EBENEEZER) Better go let Granny Setter know.

(EBENEEZER EXITS into the cabin.)

HYRAM: That Little Parson's not that little kid who used to come preaching through here with his father?

HOMER: Yup, same one. He's got the *Holy Tone,* all right. Heard him preach the side off a barn when he was nigh five years old.

(HOMER takes a swig of moonshine.)

THISBE: He's coming down the trail, there. Homer, you better hide that jug. That little fella can sure unleash the Devil's wrath.

HOMER: (Hiding the jug, amused) Reverend Fobidiah. Fo-bid-ya!

(GRANNY has ENTERED the porch from the cabin. She is carrying the *marrying rope.*)

GRANNY: (Looking towards the approaching Parson) Lord help us if we don't have some *forbiddin'* in our lives. (Calling into the house) Come on out ladies! The Little Parson's here!

(THE WOMEN EXIT the cabin and stand on the porch. FATE's hair is bedecked with wildflowers. POLLY is helping FATE straighten her gown. FATE smiles at HYRAM, who is visibly smitten by her aura.)

THADIUS: (Whispering to HYRAM) Got myself a real prize there, don't I brother?

(FOBIDIAH ENTERS. He is wearing a large-brimmed black hat and preacher's black frock-coat. He comes up the steps and takes FATE's hand, leading her over to the *marrying tree*--the large hemlock pine tree growing in Thadius' yard:)

FOBIDIAH: A radiant bride to stand before the Lord!

POLLY: Amen, Reverend.

FOBIDIAH: A new life's beginning here today.

POLLY: (Joyfully) A new life!

(The GROUP has followed FOBIDIAH to the base of the hemlock. FOBIDIAH climbs atop the tree stump, which becomes his pulpit:)

FOBIDIAH: Granny, 'tis time for the marrying rope.

GRANNY: (Holding up the rope) Here 'tis!

FOBIDIAH: Christians, take up the marrying rope! Gents on the left. Ladies on the right.

(GUITAR, DULCIMER, BANJO, FIDDLES, JEW'S HARPS twang rhythmically as the GROUP claps in rhythm and begins joining in the ritualistic wedding dance. To begin, GRANNY hands FATE one end of the rope and THADIUS the other. The MEN and WOMEN take up their respective sides of the rope and join in the dance around the hemlock tree, weaving in and out, until a series of knots are tied. HOMER is cheering the group from his porch rocker:)

HOMER: (Shouting above the music) Raise a storm cloud! Tie that wedding rope! Tie it good

(The GROUP is weaving the final knot around both THADIUS and FATE. THADIUS towers over FATE, looking down at her, intensely. THADIUS lifts FATE up onto the tree stump, beside FOBIDIAH. THADIUS rejoins the dancing. FATE looks out at HYRAM. Their gazes lock upon each other for one unnaturally prolonged BEAT. Abruptly, FOBIDIAH interrupts the action:)

FOBIDIAH: Wedding knot's tied! Let no man or woman tear it asunder!

GROUP: No man or woman, Lord!

FOBIDIAH: (Voice lowering, reverentially) Let us begin.

(The ROPE is set down around TWO CHAIRS where FATE and THADIUS are seated directly beneath FOBIDIAH's tree stump lectern. When FOBIDIAH preaches in "*The Holy Tone*," his young voice will occasionally break. His speech is unceasing and is interspersed with "ahhhs", "uhhhs", and short audible gasps of breath.)

FOBIDIAH: (Continuing, Gazing up at the tree overhead) This here hemlock's witnessed nigh three generations of mountainfolk's marryings. Ever since our great-granddaddies come over from across the wide, wide seas. All the way from Ireland.

GRANNY: And, Scotsland, too!

GROUP: Amen!

(FOBIDIAH ceremoniously opens his BIBLE, under the reverential stares of the assembled MOUNTAINFOLK.)

FOBIDIAH: Thy cursed horse-leeches of the Excise, You that make the *whiskey stills* your prize!

(The ASSEMBLED GROUP GASPS--WOMEN's hands cover their mouths--as ALL HEADS TURN fearfully TOWARDS THADIUS. THADIUS begins to bristle, straining to control himself, emitting

AUDIBLE GRUNTS as FOBIDIAH's invective against moon-shining continues.)

FOBIDIAH: (Continuing) Hold up thy hand, Devil! (Directly to THADIUS) Once, twice, thrice! There seize the blinders! And bake them up in brimstone pie for poor darn'd drinkers. Forgive them for they know not what they do, . . . oh Lord!

(THADIUS STANDS, causing the MOUNTAINFOLK to STEP BACKWARDS IN FEAR that he may perpetrate some act of violence against FOBIDIAH. After several TENSE BEATS, in which THADIUS and FOBIDIAH exchange heated looks--A STARING CONTEST!-- THADIUS looks down and kicks the dirt with his foot:)

THADIUS: What the heck! They's only words. *Forgive thy sinners, Lord.*

GROUP: (Relieved) Amen!

(THADIUS retakes his seat. The mortified FOBIDIAH WIPES his brow, relieved.)

FOBIDIAH: Thank the Lord!

GRANNY: Amen, Jesus!

(FOBIDIAH turns to FATE, and preaches up a storm. He clears his throat, then lets the invective fly:)

FOBIDIAH: And Sisters, let us not forget the tale of Potiphar's Wife. A wicked adulteress. Cursed 'til the end of time. Cursed 'til the last sun does raise its head over these Smoky Blue highlands of ours for the last Judgment Day. She was a *wicked* woman, cursed by man and beast. Consumed by the hell-fires of unbridled *passion*. CURSED 'til the end of time!

(ALL HEADS TURN towards POLLY. She receives the incriminating stares with shocked embarrassment.)

ARMINTA: Tell us the story, Reverend.

THISBE: (Sternly) Daughter, hold your tongue!

FOBIDIAH: The girl's right to be asking. We should hear the tale about that wicked woman. That *adulterating wife* of Pharoah's right hand man. She *lusted* for a lad called Joseph, who was a slave in Egypt land.

GRANNY: A slave in Egypt land. Amen!

GROUP: Amen.

FOBIDIAH: Joseph went to prison, but that *woman* fried in Hell. Listen all women who hear this tale and heed that judgment bell!

HOMER: Heed that judgment bell!

(The Revival Meeting hysteria mounts as the
GROUP chimes in AD-LIBBING "*Amen*" and
"*Lord*".)

GRANNY: *Hallelujah*, Lord!

GROUP: *Hallelujah*!

FOBIDIAH: That chain begun with Potiphar's Wife
has come down unto this land. Careful now you
pretty gals, you heed the Lord's command!

ARBYZENA: (Singing out) Heed the Lord's
command!

FOBIDIAH: The Lord hath mercy. But, not for
adulterers.

MANUEL: (A searing look to POLLY)
No *adulterers*, Lord!

FOBIDIAH: The Lord hath mercy. But, not for
those who forget their marriage vows.

GROUP: Not for them, Lord!

FOBIDIAH: (Motioning as he speaks) Rise now,
Sister Fate O'Dare. And you rise before the Lord,
Thadius Steed. The marriage vows are now
decreed by me, the Parson of the Hills. Since
childhood was I blessed by the breath of the Lord

speakin' through my soul, and bringing me to you poor *sinners*.

GRANNY: Have mercy on us *sinners*, Lord!

GROUP: *Mercy*!

FOBIDIAH: Where's the parchment?

MANUEL: (Handing parchment to FOBIDIAH) Here, Reverend.

FOBIDIAH: (Scanning the parchment) Mmmmmmmm. Good.

(When FOBIDIAH READS THE PARCHMENT, the GROUP will respond to each item with "oous" and "ahhs". And, MANUEL will receive their admiring stares with a stoic, poker face.)

FOBIDIAH: (Continuing, Reading the parchment aloud) One prize milch cow. One feather bed. Two New Hampshire laying hens. And one patchwork quilt from Manuel O'Dare are given thee, Thadius Steed, along with his little girl here. His one and only child, Fate O'Dare.

THADIUS (Pinching FATE's cheek) Sounds good to me. Mighty good.

FOBIDIAH: (Clearing his throat) Agreeable to thee, Thadius Steed?

THADIUS: (Brusquely, slapping MANUEL's back) Agreed.

FOBIDIAH: (To FATE) To love and to cherish this man who'll keep a roof over your head and firewood in the bin--

THADIUS: (Unable to resist the sexual innuendo) *Firewood* in *her bin.*

FOBIDIAH: (Trying to maintain decorum) Do you, Fate O'Dare, agree to take care of this man in sickness and in health, to stand by his side ' til death sets you apart?

FATE: (Overcome by shyness, with difficulty) I do.

FOBIDIAH: Now, speak up girl, so's we all can hear!

FATE: (Loudly) I says,...I do!

(THADIUS throws his hat into the air and emits a loud bear hoot:)

THADIUS: Rrrrrrrrrraaaaaaaaaaaaaaah!

(THADIUS KISSES FATE ON THE MOUTH, holding her so tightly against him that her back is forced to arch backwards with her head practically touching the ground. The GROUP MARKS THE

LONG BEATS with a long "*Ahhhhhh*" and exclaims "*Weee*!" when the kiss if finally completed. THE MUSICIANS break into a spirited reprise of their frenzied playing. GUESTS are converging on the banquet table.)

THADIUS: (Gesturing towards HYRAM)
Brother! Come on over here and kiss my little bride.

(HYRAM comes over to FATE and THADIUS. He stands staring awkwardly at FATE.)

THADIUS: (Continuing, Impatiently shoving HYRAM towards FATE) Didn't they learn you nothing in that *citified* school? Go on! Cause I'm only giving you permission this *one time*.

(HYRAM gently kisses FATE's cheek.)

HYRAM: Welcome to the family.

FATE: (Blushing) Thank you, Hyram Steed.

HYRAM: My sister-in-law's voice is as sweet as that gentle breeze pouring through the hemlock tree.

THADIUS: (Disappointedly, to Hyram) Hell, brother! Still playin' with the sounds of dumbfangled words! Don't never get you nothin' but wasted breath. You ain't changed none after all that schoolin'.

ARMINTA: Your brother's a *doctor*, Thadius.

(POLLY hands THADIUS a plate of food.)

THADIUS: (Eating) And watch out for *that* fillie, Brother.

ARMINTA: Your brother's a grown man, Thadius. He can take care of hisself.

THADIUS: (Ignoring ARMINTA, to HYRAM) Now go inside and shed those city duds, Hyram. You're back home, now.

ARMINTA: He looks fine to me.

THADIUS: He looks like an *outlander*. A real soft *furriner*!

HYRAM: In some ways, I may be. I feel comfortable in these clothes.

GRANNY: (Jokingly) Aw, give him a good bath in oatmeal 'n buttermilk, Thadius. That oughta bring him back to his senses.

HYRAM: A genuine *Mountain Cure*, Granny?

GRANNY: That's right. Ain't nothing better than natural cures.

ARMINTA: Why, Hyram's got hisself *book learning*. Bet he could've cured our mare last spring, after she foaled.

GRANNY: Some things just ain't meant to be. Book learning, or no.

FATE: Hyram's spent all them years studying. We gotta give him a chance.

THADIUS: My new bride's got herself a real mouthpiece on her, hasn't she? (Kissing FATE's mouth) All the tonic I need.

(FOBIDIAH has been listening. He gets the GROUP's attention as he begins HANDING OUT THE SHAPE NOTE HYMNALS:)

FOBIDIAH: It's time! Time for the groom to be taking his bride upstairs to the wedding bed to complete what the good Lord hath begun.

(THADIUS picks FATE up and turns to face the GROUP from the porch.)

THADIUS: (Gleeful anticipation) Sweeeeeeeeet Jesus!

THISBE: Have yourself one fandangle of a *shivaree*, Thadius. If'n you know what I mean.

ARBYZENA: (Sternly, to THISBE) Husband!

THISBE: It's writ in the Bible, Arbyzena. Just what d'ya think Adam 'n Eve was *doing* all that time out in that garden?

ARBYZENA: (At the end of her rope) Come here and sing the hymn, before the Devil whups you good!

THADIUS: (Chuckling) Night all!

(THADIUS EXITS indoors with FATE in his arms. THE MOUNTAINFOLK assemble around the porch. FOBIDIAH CONDUCTS THEIR HYMN SINGING:)

FOBIDIAH: The shapes! Let us sing the shapes.

GROUP: (A capella SINGING) Fa-la-do. Do-me-so. So-re-me.

(The MOUNTAINFOLK REPEAT the hymn adding harmonies.)

FOBIDIAH: That's the way the good Lord meant for his children to sing. Pure and simple. Now, let us sing the poetry.

(NOTE: Original MUSIC is available for
"SOMETIMES GOOD." MUSIC by Barbara
Rottman with LYRICS by Lichtman /Rottman.)

GROUP: (Singing) *Sometimes work, sometimes*
play; Man and woman go on your way;
Bless the night and hope each day
Sometimes good, sometimes.
Sometimes sun, sometimes storm,
A little time, and lovin's born,
Find the rose, forget the thorn;
Sometimes good, sometimes.

(THE MUSIC CONTINUES as the CYCLORAMA
takes on shades of sunset, then, night's blue-black
hues. The MOUNTAINFOLK gradually EXIT.
Only LEM, HOMER, and MANUEL remain on the
porch steps, drunkenly passing the jug back and forth
until they fall asleep snoring, contentedly.
FIREFLIES are seen in the woods--illuminated
iridescent lights on the ends of sticks.)

SCENE FOUR

*The LIGHTS COME UP on
the BEDROOM of THADIUS STEED.
THADIUS, in long-johns, is lying propped up
in bed with his elbows behind his head. He
watches FATE undress underneath her robe.
She is shy and nervous.*

FATE: Can I turn the lamp down, Thadius?

THADIUS: What fer?

FATE: (Remaining in her robe) Ain't never taken off
my clothes in front of a man before--

(THADIUS stands, moves behind FATE,
pressing himself against her.)

THADIUS: Rrrrrraaaaaah!

MEN ON THE PORCH (OFF-STAGE): (Cat-
calling, then breaking into laughter) Little bride,
little bride, NO PLACE LEFT FOR YOU TO HIDE!

(FATE is shivering with fear, obviously unnerved by
the MEN's lewdness.)

THADIUS: (Shouting to the MEN on the porch)
Hey! Shut your traps out there! (To FATE) You

ain't cold? (Wrapping his arms around her) Don't
you pay them no mind. Ya hear me?

(FATE, unable to speak, shakes her head *Yes*.)

MEN (OFF-STAGE): (Chortling, knocking on the
window) What's takin' so long?

THADIUS: (Fondling her breasts) Mmmmmm, nice
little titties. Velveteen. And all mine!

FATE: *Mine*!

 THADIUS: Gettin' all fired up, are ya?

FATE: They're mine! One person can't own another.

THADIUS: Yah? Well, you're my woman. And,
don't you never forget it.   Rrrrraaaaaaah!

(THADIUS PICKS FATE UP and DROPS HER on
the bed. BLACK OUT.)

MEN (OFF-STAGE): (Rhythmic cheers in the
BLACK OUT, mirroring the carnal act) Rah! Rah!
Rah! Rah! . . .

(In the BLACK OUT FATE SCREAMS IN PAIN, as
THADIUS SHOUTS.)

THADIUS' VOICE: (Jubilantly) She's mine now,
Loooooooorrrrrrd!

54

MEN (OFF-STAGE): (Cheering in the BLACK OUT, as though another bear has been slain) Got her! Yeah!

(BLACK OUT CONTINUES.)

SCENE FIVE
The LIGHTS COME UP on LEM, HOMER, and MANUEL snoring loudly on the front porch. The CYCLORAMA CHANGES from the DARK COLORS of NIGHT to the LIGHT OF BURNT ORANGE SUNRISE. TWO GUNSHOTS RING OUT, arousing the sleeping MEN. HOMER sits up in his rocker, listening.
TWO MORE SIGNAL SHOTS SOUND.

HOMER: (Alarmed) What's that?

(LEM is getting to his feet. TWO MORE SHOTS RING OUT.)

LEM: Signal shots!

MANUEL: Revenuers!

(THADIUS ENTERS the porch from the cabin, pulling on his overalls.)

THADIUS: Those're Uriah's signal shots.

HOMER: Been after ya ever since ya shot up that last Revenuer, Nephew.

LEM: What d'ya want us to do, Thadius?

THADIUS: Nothing, Lem. It's me they're after. I gotta hightail it outa here.

MANUEL: You gonna cross the line to Virginia?

THADIUS: Yup. Like I done last time. 'Til they let up some.

FATE (OFF-STAGE): (Scared) Thadius?

THADIUS: Hell! Last time I had to hide myself working in that coal mine for nigh six months. Place is ugly. Ain't no place to be taking that little filly of mine.

HOMER: Ya gotta travel light. We'll take care of Fate 'til it's safe for you to come back home again, Thadius. Feds'll watch her close, once they find out you two're hitched.

 (HYRAM ENTERS from S.R., brushing hay off his clothes.)

HYRAM: (Yawning) What's going on?

THADIUS: Damned bloodhound Revenuers're after me.

HYRAM: What can I do to help you, Thadius?

THADIUS: A pack of mountain lions couldn't tear me from my filly right now, but I don't favor penitentiaries none. I gotta hide out in Virginia. I need to know you'll be taking care of my little gal fer me, while I'm gone.

HYRAM: Of course I will.

THADIUS: Take care of her like she was your own--

(FATE ENTERS the porch from the cabin. She is barefooted, wearing a robe, and is ashen-faced and emotionally drained.)

FATE: (Struggling to get the words out) What . . . What's happenin'? Some . . . Something wr . . . wrong?

HYRAM: Don't worry, Thadius. I'll watch her for you.

FATE: *Wa . . .watch me?* Wh . . .what've I done?

THADIUS: Gotta leave here for a while.

FATE: (Doesn't process, is she leaving too?) Leave? . . .Leave? You want me to . . .to LEAVE?

(FATE uncontrollably BREAKS DOWN IN TEARS, overcome by what has happened to her and the toll that it has taken on her ability to function.)

MANUEL: Not you, girl. Revenuers're after Thadius. He's the one whose gotta get outa here.

THADIUS: (Taking hold of FATE's shoulders, roughly SHAKING HER) No wife of Thadius Steed's blubbers like a weak babe when trouble shows her face around here.

HYRAM: (Alarmed by THADIUS' physical abuse of FATE) Easy there, Thad. She's looking unwell.

THADIUS: (Ignoring HYRAM, grabs FATE's arm) D'ya hear me. gal?

FATE: (Numbed) I . . .I hear.

THADIUS: (Releasing FATE from his grasp) It's your wifely duty to tend to things here 'til I get back. Understand? Now, hurry and pack my things.

(Rubbing her sore arm, FATE EXITS into the cabin. THREE SHOTS RING OUT.)

MANUEL: (Calling in to FATE) Hurry the packing, girl! They're crossing over the bald.

LEM: (Handing THADIUS a rifle) Loaded it for ya, Thad.

THADIUS: Much obliged. Hope I don't have to use it.

HYRAM: We'll stall them for as long as we can, when they get here.

58

(FATE ENTERS the porch from the cabin. She is carrying a small duffle bag and a sack with food.)

FATE: (Handing the provisions to THADIUS) Wed . . . wed . . . wedding vittles.

(THADIUS takes the bags and slaps FATE's backside. She struggles to remain composed. THADIUS strides over to HYRAM, resolutely extending his HAND TOWARDS HYRAM's:)

THADIUS: I'm countin' on you brother to take care of that little filly of mine.

HYRAM: I promise you, I will.

(HYRAM and THADIUS' ARMS INTERLOCK in an ARM-WRESTLE-LIKE CLENCH, sealing the bargain.

BLACK OUT.)

END OF ACT ONE.

ACT TWO
SCENE ONE

*The LIGHTS COME UP
on the narrow tunnel of a COAL MINE.
MEN are swinging pick-axes, laboring.
THADIUS joins the crew, wearing a
hardhat with oil lamplight affixed to it.
A LOUD WHISTLE BLOWS. The work
ceases. THADIUS lays his pick down
and sits down beside a sickly looking
coal miner, ORVAL SPEAR. ORVAL is
coughing into his handkerchief.*

MALE VOICE (OFF-STAGE): Break! Break time!

CASEY: Not one minute too soon.

THADIUS: Coughing up your guts, Orval.

ORVAL: Black lung gets us all sooner or later.

THADIUS: You gotta quit this place.

ORVAL: (Coughing) Quit! With three kids at home and another on the way?

THADIUS: The Coal Company's gotta provide--

ORVAL: *Provide*! That's some fancy big word.

CASEY: Why, Hell, they don't even *provide* the coffins 't bury us in.

(THE WHISTLE BLOWS again. The MEN pick up their axes and begin working.)

THADIUS: Ain't right.

ORVAL: 'Course it ain't. Nancy said a letter came for you yesterday. From your wife?

THADIUS: Yah. Little Parson brung it to me.

ORVAL: You know how to read?

THADIUS: Sure do. I was always the class bully, but I went to our little mountain school house through 6th grade. Wish I was back home. Who'd ever have thought I'd be here this long?

ORVAL: Why hell, you only been here 7 months. I been here 12 years. What did your little woman have to say?

THADIUS: Says our child's growing inside her.

ORVAL: Real happy for ya, Thad.

THADIUS: But, there was something else in that letter.

ORVAL: What was it?

THADIUS: More what she didn't say. And in that Little Parson's eyes when he told me he'd hoped I'd be home soon to *'take charge of my family.'* (Swinging his axe) Damn!

(BLACK OUT.)

SCENE TWO
The setting is the same as Scene 1, Act I.
It is late November of 1910.
FATE and HYRAM have climbed to the top of FATE's hill (S.L.) to watch the sun rise.
FATE is six months pregnant.
As FATE and HYRAM are bathed in the sunrise glow, they sit side-by-side listening to the BIRDS.

FATE: Sun rise is special up here.

HYRAM: Autumn's radiant colors warm the heart, don't they?

FATE: *Radiant?* Don't know that word.

HYRAM: *Radiant* is the shimmering of the sun on the river.

FATE: (Savoring the word) *Radiant! . . .Radiant!*

HYRAM: Or the snow-capped mountain peaks *radiantly glowing* in the sunlight.

FATE: It's hard to believe seven months have passed since my wedding day. And, seven months Thadius's child's been growing inside my body. Nothing makes sense to me. I'm so . . . confused.

HYRAM: Feelings are natural for a woman in your condition Fate. Medical jargon would call it *hormones*.

FATE: I'm taking a whole different look at life, now.

HYRAM: Down below us, there. That's life in all of its struggle and splendor. Cataloochee Cove. The church. The cemetery. The hand-hewn cabins. The fields standing out against the hillsides.

FATE: Why must we struggle so? Why, when I look down upon our Cove cemetery and think of all the younguns we had here last Fall, it nigh breaks my heart. Measles took all the Bohanan's wee ones, and Hettie Ownby's sweet little Abraham.

HYRAM: (Looking out upon the community below) Death needs no apology here.

FATE: We're all *colors* in a patchwork quilt

HYRAM: Yes. Each one of us is part of the divine scheme.

FATE: Hyram, ever since I was a youngun, all we had in our home was a terrible silence. I never knew how beautiful *words* could be until I heard you speaking them. Why, you put into words all the things I feel deep down inside.

HYRAM: Guess I've found a fellow poetry-lover in you, dear sister-in-law.

FATE: Tell me that poem about the sea.

HYRAM: Edgar Allan Poe's?

FATE: Uhuh. The one who writ all them hant stories.

HYRAM: *'For the moon never beams without bringing me dreams of the beautiful Anabelle Lee....'*

FATE: (Purring, contentedly) Mmmmmmmmmmmmmmmm. Go on.

HYRAM: *'And the stars never rise, but I feel the bright eyes of the beautiful Anabelle Lee. . . .'*

FATE: Go on.

HYRAM: *'And so all the night tide I lie down by the side of my darling, my darling, my wife and my bride, in her sepulcher there by the sea, in her tomb by the sounding sea.'*

(THE SHADOW OF A BIRD WASHES OVER THEM. Its CALL diverts their attention. ARMINTA ENTERS, hiding behind a tree, spying on FATE and HYRAM.)

FATE: How I'd like to fly there.

HYRAM: Like an angel.

FATE: The sea. How does it sound?

HYRAM: Like the wind moving through those leaves beneath us.

FATE: (Passions mounting) I know how the sea feels, then. Hold me?

HYRAM: (Fighting to control his own passions) You know we can't. Thadius has supported me all these years. And, ever since I can remember, all I've ever wanted was to be a doctor, so I could help our mountainfolk. Prevent some of those prematurely dug graves down there. They're just starting to trust me a little. Beginning to come to me for advice.

FATE: They know you can help them.

HYRAM: They're Christians, Fate. The things you and I are feeling are sinful in their eyes. You belong to someone else.

(ARMINTA EXITS, undetected.)

FATE: I've read the Bible. The things you and me're feeling aren't sins.

HYRAM: You've always had music in your soul.

FATE: (Paraphrasing Solomon) *My beloved is mine and I am his.*

HYRAM: No, Fate!

FATE: (Moving closer to him, continuing)
My beloved take me, as the little foxes that spoil the vines. (Placing HYRAM's hand on her breast)
For my vines have tender grapes that'll surely burst open with wanting.

HYRAM: (Speaking with urgency) I'll have to speak with Thadius.

FATE: (Afraid) He'll hurt you if he knows.

HYRAM: We cannot pretend any longer --

 (HYRAM EMBRACES FATE, aroused. The two of them lower themselves to their knees, embracing. As their hands trace each other's body, their breathing accelerates.)

HYRAM: Dear God! What'll we do?

FATE: (Suddenly, grabbing her stomach) Ouch!

HYRAM: (Concerned) Fate?

FATE: The baby. It kicked me!

(HYRAM places his hand on FATE's stomach, feeling the BABY KICK again, as FATE gasps.)

HYRAM: Yes! I can feel it now, too!

 (HYRAM and FATE break into LAUGHTER, like two children making a wonderful discovery. HYRAM takes FATE in his arms and kisses her, passionately.

BLACK OUT.)

SCENE THREE

The LIGHTS COME UP
on the Steed's cabin, the same setting as
Act 1, Scene 3. A late autumn CORN
HUSKING gathering is winding down.
The MOUNTAINFOLK are all present--
the OGLES, OWNBYS, STEEDS,
O'DARES, GRANNY, and FOBIDIAH.
WOMEN are stripping kernels from
corn husks as they stand conversing
around the husking tables.
MENFOLK are sorting the harvested
corn into bins situated alongside the
husking tables. The entire community is
actively at work.
UNCLE HOMER is making the wood-
jointed LIMBERJACK DOLL DANCE
ON ITS WOODEN BOARD,
entertaining the CHILDREN.

A WILD HOOT issues forth from
ARMINTA OGLE, whose found
the PRIZED RED CORN HUSK.

ARMINTA: (Holding up the prized RED CORN HUSK) It's mine! The RED ONE!

HOMER: (To THISBE) Got yourself one lucky gal, there, Thisbe Ogle.

THISBE: Her time might finally be coming.

ARMINTA: Ever since I was youngun', I always hoped I'd get me mine.

FOBIDIAH: Finding the red corn husk means, after the husking's done, you getta pick any single fella to be your *Corn Husking King.*

(HOMER diverts the GROUP's attention with his LIMBERJACK DOLL antics. The GROUP GATHERS AROUND THE PORCH, watching the dancing doll.)

HOMER: (Sing-songey, making DOLL DANCE) Limberjack, limberjack, may look like nonsense but he's more than that. Yes, he's more than that.

(EVERYONE APPLAUDS HOMER's entertainment. The MOUNTAINFOLK return to the husking tables.)

HETTIE: (Wistfully, to LEM) Remember how our little Abraham used to tell us how he'd seen Uncle Homer's limberjack man taking hisself a stroll in the moonlight?

LEM: (Covering HETTIE's hand with his, strolling away from the porch with her) Some things we'll never forget.

(HYRAM takes FATE's hand, leading her towards the tables. FOBIDIAH watches them with visible disapproval, as he takes a seat on the porch beside HOMER.)

FOBIDIAH: You and that little man of yours know what's been going on here, Uncle Homer. And keeping mum ain't what the Lord had in mind when he commanded us to keep His *Ten Golden Rules*.

HOMER: Some things are best to be let alone, Reverend.

FOBIDIAH: Well, I best be gettin' on my way if'n I'm gonna make it over to see Thadius tomorrow.

HOMER: Drop by this way before you leave. Fate'll be wantin' to send Thadius a fresh bread she's baked special for him.

(FOBIDIAH leaves the porch and wends his way over to the husking table, eavesdropping on the WOMEN's gossip, as they work.)

ARBYZENA: Fate 'n him 're always together. Never seen 'em apart.

GRANNY: Thadius ain't dumb. Menfolk got themselves a sixth sense when it comes to womenfolk strayin' from the nest.

HETTIE: Thadius has got hisself the nose of a grizzley bar.

ARMINTA: But, Thadius asked Hyram to keep an eye on Fate for him.

ARBYZENA: An *EYE*, he said.

(FOBIDIAH clears his throat, making his presence known. He tips his hat, moving towards the eating table:)

FOBIDIAH: Afternoon, ladies. Busy hands make for happy souls.

GRANNY: Amen, Reverend.

(ARMINTA stares wistfully towards HYRAM, who is sorting the husks.)

ARMINTA: Ain't too many fellas get asked to be *Corn Husking King*. Things can change.

MANUEL: (Standing on a stool, calling) Husking's all done!

(ARMINTA goes to HYRAM's side:)

ARMINTA: Hyram Steed, will you be my *Corn Husking King*?

70

(HYRAM darts an instantaneous questioning glance towards FATE, before bowing regally to ARMINTA:)

HYRAM: Why,...why I'd be honored, Miss Arminta Ogle.

(HYRAM and ARMINTA lead the procession to the dinner table, where they are both crowned and are seated.
THE LIGHTS DIM on THE MOUNTAINFOLK seated at the table, as a BLUE LIGHT SPECIAL illuminates HOMER.)

HOMER: (To the AUDIENCE, speaking his mind) Chewing the fat is good for the soul. We mountainfolk work hard, but we also like to sit down to a good meal together after the long times of bein' alone in our coves and hollers. So's we can see things like they are. Worried about what's been happening here since Thadius left. Why that brother of his is as soft-boiled as Thadius is hard. No middle ground betwixt them. (Holding LIMBERJACK DOLL UP, addressing it) We sure can feel the storm 'abrewing, can't we little man? Thunder 'n lightning, and . . . tears.

(THE LIGHTS COME UP slightly on the supper scene, as the meal progresses in pantomimed fashion.
THE LIGHTING FAVORS THE PORCH. FATE wanders over to HOMER, sitting on the top step.)

HOMER: Ain't you joinin' the others?

FATE: Nope. Not hungry. Feeling low all-of-a-sudden.

HOMER: Missing your *husband*?

FATE: (Avoiding the question) Tell me one of your tall tales, Uncle Homer.

HOMER: Girl, you shouldn't be needin' any pick-yew-ups. The Little Parson's bringing word to Thadius it's okay to for him to come on home. Why, you oughta be downright glad your husband's coming home any day, now.

FATE: Maybe it's just the first sign of winter giving me these *blue* feelings. Why, there was ice on the sill this morning. Your storytelling's the best cure-all we got.

HOMER: Mmmmm. I'll tell you the tale of *The Witch Hantin' of Rattlesnake Holler*.

FATE: Never keered much for that place. Always smelt like something was dyin' there.

HOMER: You can ask Granny Setter. She'd remember that Cherokee woman who came through here during a bad storm. Long before Thadius 'er any of you was borned. Said she had magic charms....Well, they was real poor, this family livin' down in the holler in them days. Didn't know nothin' about puttin' witch hobble leaves over their doors or above their fireplace. That Cherokee woman come 'aknocking at the door. When the woman of the house seen the Injun outside in the blizzard, she strung the latch, 'afeared she was goin' to be kilt....Many hours that miserable Injun gal waited outside the door pleading. 'Til the man of the house come home and found her near froze to death....

FATE: Pa's daddy lost four toes, 'cause of the frostbite.

HOMER: Frostbite's a miserable curse. Being a good Christian, and knowing there was only one proper way for him to act, the man of the house brung that Injun woman inside. His wife would have no part of the deed, however.
When the daylight come and the storm passed, the Cherokee was ready to take her leave. She took a large kernel of corn from her pouch and gave it to the man of the house, sayin', *'Plant this here corn and it'll bring yew much wealth.'* But, to the man's wife, that Cherokee woman looked snake-eyed and let fly a dreadful curse: *'Until I am dead and buried in the ground, you will suffer with the rheumatiz. The dampness'll cling to your bones, the way it done to mine lyin' outside your door in that miserable cold.'*

(HOMER stops speaking. He takes several long puffs on his corn-cob pipe.)

FATE: Lord-a-mercy, Uncle Homer! What
happened to them folks? Did the Cherokee woman's
prophecy come to be?

HOMER: Yup.

FATE: Stop teasin' and tell me what happened.

HOMER: Hooked myself another good catch, hev I?

FATE: Tell me, Uncle!

HOMER: Well, come spring, that mountain man
planted that magic corn kernel on his land. Come
summer, it was nigh as high as the top of the gap.
Tickling the sky and sprouting corn that was so big, it
took two men to lift one shuck.

FATE: You're joshin' me!

HOMER: The wife. Well, that was no happy story.

FATE: Did she die?

HOMER: Worse. She suffered with the *rheumatiz*
for 'nigh twenty years. Shriveled up like some apple
doll twice't her age. 'Til that Cherokee woman joined
her Maker. Only then, did that mountain woman
unbend and swear never, never to do an
unChristian deed. (Moralizing, pointedly to FATE)
That wife learned her lesson the hard way, girl. She
learned that when the husband ain't to home, it's the
woman's job to tend to the God-fearing ways. To
uphold *The Ten Golden Rules*.

(LIGHTS COME UP ON THE TABLE, where the action resumes.
HYRAM CALLS TOWARDS FATE, HOLDING UP A PLATE:)

HYRAM: Fate, strawberry pie!

FATE: (Rising, to join HYRAM, calling out to him) Just what I've been hankering for. (FATE is stopped briefly by HOMER's warning look, before she joins the others at the supper table. FOBIDIAH rises, to make a blessing:)

FOBIDIAH: (Clears his throat, eyeing FATE) Let us bow our heads. We thank thee Lord for your bounteous harvest. For the delectable food our womenfolk prepared for this golden harvest celebration.... (Darting HYRAM a piercing glare) We good Christians swear to uphold your *Golden Rules. ALL TEN OF THEM*!

GRANNY: *Golden Rules*, Lord!

GROUP: Amen. We swear!

(The tension is mounting between HYRAM and FATE, as FOBIDIAH's searing eye falls upon FATE, who shifts uncomfortably in her chair, feeling the heat of accusation rising.)

FOBIDIAH: *Sinners*, take heed!

HOMER: Take heed!

FOBIDIAH: (Eyes closed, head turned heavenwards) Forsake us not, oh Lord. Do *not* forsake us. Amen.

GROUP: Amen.

 (FOBIDIAH puts his broad-rimmed black hat on and begins to EXIT.)

FOBIDIAH: Best I get moving, if I'm gonna reach Thadius by tomorrow.

GRANNY: (Handing lunch pail with food to FOBIDIAH) Take these vittles for your journey, Reverend.

FOBIDIAH: (Inhaling the contents of the pail) Mmmmmm. Mighty neighborly, Sister Setter.

LEM: Tell Thadius we all been missing him.

(FATE steps forward with a loaf of bread wrapped in a cloth.)

FATE: (Handing bread to FOBIDIAH) Give this to Thadius for me, Reverend. Tell him I baked it fresh this morning.

FOBIDIAH: (Searching FATE's eyes, as though trying to lance a boil) Anything you wanna be saying to your *husband*, Sister Steed?

(THE MOUNTAINFOLKS' EYES are riveted upon FATE.)

FATE: Tell him,...tell Thadius,...tell my husband that I...that I hope he's well.

FOBIDIAH: That *all* you care to tell him?

FATE: And...that...that we--

FOBIDIAH: (Trapping her) That *you*, his *wife*, Fate O'Dare Steed. You're hankerin' to have him home with you?

FATE: (Weakly) Yes, Reverend.

(FATE returns to the picnic table with the MOUNTAINFOLK. The LIGHTS DIM on the picnic table, as a BLUE LIGHT SPECIAL once again picks up HOMER'S PORCH ROCKER. FOBIDIAH stops near the porch, where HOMER is in his rocker savoring the home-baked delicacies, despite his toothless state.)

FOBIDIAH: Still prefer to eat alone, I see, Uncle Homer.

HOMER: Wish I had me a pair of them *Roebuckers*.

FOBIDIAH: Heard them store-bought ones work real good.

HOMER: Maybe Thadius can bring me back a pair?

FOBIDIAH: I'll mention it to him. (Holding up FATE'S bread) Even when the chewing's hard, Lord, the truth must be swallowed!

(FOBIDIAH EXITS. HOMER is worried, as he speaks to the LIMBERJACK DOLL:)

HOMER: (Confidentially) You 'n me, we can feel the storm 'abrewing, can't we little man?

(HOMER makes the LIMBERJACK DANCE. A GIANT LIMBERJACK'S SHADOW DANCES UPON THE CYCLORAMA, its arms and legs swinging wildly. The CASTANET-LIKE SOUNDS of the LIMBERJACK SWELL IN VOLUME. BLACK OUT.)

SCENE FOUR

It is dinner time in the West Virginia home of the miner ORVAL SPEAR. The one-room hovel houses ORVAL, his pregnant wife NANCY, their TWO CHILDREN, and THADIUS. ALL are SEATED at a barren dinner table. NANCY ladles out thin soup into tin bowls.

ORVAL: (Saying Grace before the meal)
Lord, we thank you for what we have. We ask you to bless our good friend, Thadius Steed, here. We ask you to make it safe so he can go back to his own family real soon.

78

FAMILY & THADIUS: Amen.

ORVAL: (To THADIUS) Sorry the dinner ain't much, but it's all we got, Thadius.

THADIUS: Appreciate the hospitality 'n all. Thanks, Nancy.

NANCY: Imagine you're missing a real home-cooked meal, and...*family*.

THADIUS: Miss my place something fierce. My little wife's belly must be big as yours by now. Expectin' The Little Parson here with some word any day now.

ORVAL: Must be some sight, those Smoky Mountains of yours.

THADIUS: Best sight the Lord could ever give us mortals. Makes a man feel Godlike, just bein' there.

NANCY: A sight prettier than this soot-stained town of ours.

THADIUS: Wish Orval and you and the kids could come back with me.

ORVAL: Sure we'd all like that right fine. Only I can't spare the time off right now. Maybe, someday.

THADIUS: Someday things might be better right here. Once we get that *union* of yours up and running.

ORVAL: If they don't fire us all first.

NANCY: It all scares me.

THADIUS: It's the only way these men here can live like they's men, 'stead of over-burdened pack mules, killing themselves for less than living wages.

ORVAL: Health benefits, too, Nancy. Thadius says we oughta' have 'em.

THADIUS: Course you should. The Company's gotta provide--

(THADIUS is interrupted by a KNOCKING AT THE DOOR. NANCY goes to open the door. FOBIDIAH ENTERS, removing his hat.)

FOBIDIAH: Evening, Ma'am. I come to fetch Thadius Steed.

(THADIUS is getting to his feet.)

NANCY: Has his baby come?

FOBIDIAH: Not yet. Any time, now.
(To THADIUS) Fate baked this bread for you

THADIUS: (Handing the bread to NANCY) Something special for your dinner table.

NANCY: (Placing the bread on the table) Much thanks, Thadius.

FOBIDIAH: Revenuers 're gone. Time you headed home, Thadius. Is there someplace we can talk, private-like?

THADIUS: (Moving towards door, EXITING) Excuse us, Nancy and Orval. We can step outside, there, Reverend.

(FOBIDIAH EXITS with THADIUS. BLACK OUT.)

SCENE 5

The LIGHTS COME UP on the porch of Steed's homestead. The cyclorama reflects night's hues.
FATE and HYRAM are seated together on the steps. HYRAM's ear is on FATE's stomach.

FATE: (Giggling) You're tickling!

HYRAM: Shhhhhhhhhh.

FATE: Wild Steed blood. That's for certain.

HYRAM: I hope Thadius gets home soon.

FATE: I'm gonna tell him, Hyram--

HYRAM: No, Fate. You must let me--

 (A GUN SHOT RINGS OUT as THADIUS
ENTERS with *blood in his eye*, and obviously
drunk.)

THADIUS: (Drunkenly) That *my filly* you're
pawing all over, kid brother?

FATE: (Getting to her feet) Thadius! We gotta
talk, you 'n me--

(THADIUS FIRES A SHOT, closely missing
HYRAM and hitting the SHIP'S BELL, making it
CLANG.
HYRAM is standing in front of FATE, protectively.)

HYRAM: No, Thadius!...For Gods' sake, your
child's inside of her.

THADIUS: (Drunkenly) Yah? Sure it's mine?

(HOMER ENTERS from the barn, S.R., brushing hay
off of his clothes. Using his walking stick, he
cautiously approaches THADIUS.)

HOMER: Nephew, you're outa your head *drunk*!

THADIUS: Since when d'you take to barn-sleepin'
with the milch cows, Uncle?

HOMER: Fate's birthin' time's gettin' closer.
Thought it best for Hyram, he being a doctor 'n all, to
be close by her--

(THADIUS FIRES A SHOT, wounding HYRAM's shoulder. HYRAM MOANS, clutching his shoulder.)

FATE: (Screams, helping HYRAM to sit on the porch) Hyram!

(THADIUS RAISES HIS GUN TOWARDS HYRAM, again. FATE STANDS BETWEEN HYRAM and THADIUS' GUN.)

THADIUS: Outa my way, woman!

FATE: No! Kill me, husband! I wish ya would right now and get it over with!

(THADIUS TRAINS HIS RIFLE ON FATE for SEVERAL TENSE BEATS before LOWERING IT.)

THADIUS: Nope. Might be killing my own seed....Mine?

FATE: Yeeeeees! I hope your damnable seed kills me just the way it done your other womenfolk.

(HOMER is examining HYRAM's wound.)

HOMER: Only grazed, but we gotta stop that bleedin'. Gotta get you inside, Nephew.

HYRAM: (Getting to his feet) The child's yours, Thadius. Leave her be.

(HYRAM EXITS indoors with HOMER. FATE remains facing THADIUS.)

THADIUS: The Little Parson said you're *Potiphar's Wife*....Adulterating bitch!

(SIGNAL SHOTS RING OUT. MANUEL, LEM, and THISBE ENTER. They are winded and sweating.)

THISBE: (Winded) They must've trailed you back here, Thadius.

(TWO MORE SIGNAL SHOTS SOUND.)

LEM: Got me twenty rounds of shot, Thad.

MANUEL: Federal Marshall crossed over the bald a short time ago.

THISBE: We'll hold 'em off for ya.

(HYRAM ENTERS from the house, his shoulder bandaged. THADIUS looks at HYRAM with blood in his eye. HOMER ENTERS the porch, standing near HYRAM. FATE is frozen on the porch step, leaning against the post.)

LEM: You've killed Feds before, Thad.

HOMER: Only he weren't drunk out 'o his head.

HYRAM: There'll be no more killings--

THADIUS: *I* give the orders here!

HYRAM: I'll turn myself in. Let them take me.

FATE: (Unable to contain herself) No!

HYRAM: I'm a Steed, too, remember. The whiskey still's as much mine as it is yours, Thadius. Only, I haven't killed anyone. The most they can give me is seven to fifteen years.

HOMER: Hyram's right about that, Thadius.

HYRAM : (EXITING into the cabin)
I'll be waiting for them when they come. Goodbye, Thadius.

(HYRAM EXITS into the cabin.)

FATE: (Desperate, to MANUEL) No, Pa! Don't let him do it!

MANUEL: (Brushing her off, with disgust)
I ain't your Pa. *Never* was.

(FATE is desperate. She is on her knees before THADIUS.)

FATE: He's your brother, Thadius. He's hurt! (Grabbing THADIUS' arm) They'll lock him up!

(THADIUS SHOVES FATE to the ground, as though she is an irritating fly, and HE SPITS DOWN AT

HER. THADIUS allows THISBE, MANUEL,
and LEM to lead him off, EXITING S.R.)

LEM: (EXITING) We gotta get you away from
here, Thadius.

FATE: (On all fours, calling after THADIUS,
pleading) Husband!

(FATE CRAWLS TO THE PORCH STEPS, where
she sits, dejectedly.
HOMER and HYRAM ENTER the porch from the
house.)

HOMER: You think they'll believe your story 'bout
you 'n Thadius feudin' and him fallin' off that
mountain bald up there ?

HYRAM: Lord knows, it wouldn't be the first blood
feud around here. That way they can take me in on
the tax evasion charge. That should satisfy them.

FATE: (Drained) You're not leavin' me, are you,
Hyram?

HYRAM: (To HOMER, gently touching FATE's
head) Send for her mother, Uncle Homer. She
shouldn't be alone, now.

FATE: (Struggling to get the words out)
You're not. . . going?

HYRAM: I've done too much harm here. Hurt
everyone I ever loved.

FATE: But, what about us?

HYRAM: You're my brother's wife. Take care of that child inside of you. Remember it's got our Steed blood running through its veins.

 (HYRAM EXITS S.L. FATE EMITS an enraged WAIL, GRABS HER STOMACH, and EXITS into the cabin, SLAMMING THE DOOR BEHIND HER. HOMER lowers his head, shaking it mournfully.

BLACK OUT.)

END OF ACT TWO.

ACT THREE

SCENE ONE
It is January of 1911.
Light streams from the windows of
Thadius' cabin. The shadows of
SQUARE DANCERS pass before the
windows as FIDDLE MUSIC and
THADIUS' VOICE stream onto the
stage.

THADIUS (OFF-STAGE): (In nasal fashion of
square-dance-caller) Eight hands up and go to the
left; half and back; that's it fillies now sash-i-ate.
First four, forwards and get you back; forward again,
you're gettin' the nack; now cage the birds gents.
Bird hop out and hoot-owl in; forgive us Lord
for our sins. Swing and circle four, settle up now or
never-more. Forward and back, then, home you go.
That's the way, now dosey doe.

 (The FIDDLE MUSIC continues, as HOMER,
using his cane, comes out onto the porch for some
fresh air. He sits in his rocker, fanning himself.)

HOMER: (Speaking to the audience) Whew! Hot
in there as a kettle 'bout to burst its lid. Baby
namings are whoopin' it up times. Even when the
creek's froze over and the birds have by-your-leave
hightailed it to warmer parts. (Inhaling deeply,
coughs, then pats his chest) Best I take my medicine.
 (HOMER kneels, removing the whiskey jug from its
porch hiding place and takes a swill, then exhales
for several beats, grinning) Feel twenty-five-years

younger already. (More seriously, indicating towards house) Youth is wasted on the foolish. Little mother in there should be *shivareeing* up a storm. Oh, she's tryin'. But I see beneath that pasted on smile of hers. I know my eyes are fadin'. But I can see where most never could. Ever since word come about Hyram being deathly ill in jail from the infection in that bullet wound Thadius give him, Fate's been pining away. Then, today, when word come that there's no hope for Hyram lasting more than a day or two, sure as the bar hibernates comes winter, I could see Fate's own candle going out,

(THADIUS' BEAR ROAR IS HEARD, followed by a BABY'S CRY. THADIUS barrels out ENTERING the porch hooting wildly, swilled with liquor, as POLLY pushes him out through the door.)

POLLY: (Lecturing THADIUS) Son-in-law, get yourself out there to cool off. You swilled enough Devil's brew to drown Noah's ark. Scarin' the livin' daylights out of your own daughter. Why, she'll grow up thinkin' she's got a grizzley bar for a daddy.
 (To HOMER) Uncle Homer, keep an eye on him 'til he sobers up some.

HOMER: I'll try, Polly. Sit yourself down, Nephew.

(POLLY EXITS indoors, closing the door behind her. THADIUS sits on the top step, bursting into a fit of LAUGHTER.)

THADIUS: (Drying tears of laugher from his eyes) Everything's going to be fine and dandy, Uncle. Next time we'll be having us a *BOY*. Mark my words. A regular bar!

HOMER: Shush yourself, Thadius. Things ain't right. We got us some talkin' to do.

THADIUS: Talking and blubberin'! What good is *words*? Words is for fools,. Damn that Hyram with all his *fancy* words.

HOMER: Don't be too quick to *damn*. Hyram's passing into the next world. He's dyin', Thadius.

THADIUS: *Damn* him!

HOMER: Hold yer tongue! You'll be plenty sorry for the things you've said and done.

THADIUS: The Hell I will! Why, d'ya see that babe in there suckin' away at that milch cow's teat?

HOMER: Fate ain't no *milch cow*. She's a *human being*.

THADIUS: Good *milch cow*. Be rearin' us a whole possle of Steeds to keep their daddy's line 'agoin'.

HOMER: Your wife's ailin'.

THADIUS: Don't got no wife. Just got me one good *milch cow* to bar me a line of Steeds.

HOMER: Then there's no way to hold back the terrible flood gates of ruin, if'n you believe that in your heart.

THADIUS: *Hearts* is for womenfolk and old men.

HOMER: That's your trouble, Thadius. Never letting yourself be the human being you was borned to be. I've done my best with you. Now, it's too late, I fear.

THADIUS: (Concerned) You ain't ailin', Uncle Homer?

HOMER: Me? Old bar breath Homer Steed? (Laughing in one single guffaw) Save your concern for them that needs it.

THADIUS: (Relieved) Kinda scared me for one minute there.

HOMER: Ain't ready to give me back to the Cherokee, yet, are ya?

THADIUS: (Teasing) Depends on what kind of a bar skin I could get myself in trade for you.

(Both MEN LAUGH for a few moments. An OWL IS HEARD HOOTING OFF-STAGE. The MEN sit in silence, listening to it.)

HOMER: You gotta stop what's happening in your home, Thadius. Before it's too late--

(HOMER is interrupted as the front door opens and LEM, HETTIE, and EBENEEZER OWNBY ENTER the porch from the house, putting on their winter coats.)

HETTIE: Button up good, Ebeneezer. I don't want you comin' down with none of your chest coughs on me again this winter.

(THADIUS gets to his feet to bid his guests farewell.)

THADIUS: Sure do appreciate you comin' to welcome our little Hope into the world.

HETTIE: *Hope*. Fine name for a youngun.

LEM: We had ourselves a good time of it, Thadius. Looks like it's gonna be a long winter.

HETTIE: She's a right pretty youngun. A flower, like her mama, she is.

THADIUS: (Overpowering HETTIE with his whiskey breath) Why, heck! Ain't she as purty as her daddy?

HETTIE: (Taking a few steps away from THADIUS) Thadius Steed, you have swilled yourself right outa your senses, if'n you think you're pretty. That child's as delicate as hand-painted china.

Just like my little Abraham was . . . before we lost him.

(HETTIE is saddened by the recollection of her own dead child. LEM touches his wife's hand, soothingly.)

LEM: No, no use upsetting yourself, Hettie.

THADIUS: Ain't I the bull in the china shop?   All brawn, no brain. Right, Lem?

LEM: Now you're talkin', Thad. Now, you're talkin'.

(THADIUS AND LEM LOCK ARMS and rest their elbows on the porch rail, as they arm wrestle. EBENEEZER looks on with excitement.)

EBENEEZER: Watch out there, Pa! He's whuppin' ya!   (LEM and THADIUS are grunting like two bears) Thadius Steed, you watch out. My Pa's gonna show you a thing 'er two. Ain't ya, Pa? Let him have it. A little more juice there!

HOMER: Thadius, you be careful. Don't go breakin' his arm.

(THADIUS GRUNTS VICTORIOUSLY, as LEM'S arm is forced down against the railing.)

THADIUS: Had your fill, brother Ownby?

(LEM is moaning loudly, as THADIUS continues to bear down on his arm.)

HETTIE: Let him be, Thadius Steed, you mountain lion! Can't you see he's hurtin'? You're breakin' his arm! (Swatting THADIUS) Let him be, I say!

(THADIUS releases LEM, who is rubbing his sore arm. THADIUS is laughing, victoriously.)

LEM: King of Steed's Holler, Thadius. King of the beasts. No denyin' it. (EXITING with his family, calls back) Thanks again' for the tasty vittles 'n all.

THADIUS: Y'all be careful fordin' the creek, ya hear?

HETTIE: (Calling back, EXITING) Goodnight, Thadius.

EBENEEZER: (Calling back, EXITING) Night, Thadius.

(THE OWNBY FAMILY EXITS S.L. FIDDLE MUSIC ceases.)

THADIUS: (Rubbing his face, thinking aloud) Maybe I am a bull in a china shop. (Looking towards the house) Two females under my roof. Seems like I can never say the right things.

HOMER: Granny Setter'll tell ya, womenfolk carry on that way after they've given birth. Just remember, she ain't no milch cow.

(THISBE, ARBYZENA, and ARMINTA ENTER the porch from the house. THISBE is having trouble walking, as he's had more whiskey than he can hold. He puts his arm around ARBYZENA'S shoulders.)

ARBYZENA: Husband! If you expect me to carry yew home, you got another thing coming.

(THISBE, a small wirey man--shorter than ARBYZENA--jumps up forcing her to catch him in her arms like a baby.)

THISBE: Ain't I *your* baby, Arbyzena, my love?

(ARBYZENA drops THISBE off the porch into a mound of snow. He digs his way out, removing he snow from his mouth.)

ARBYZENA: (To ARMINTA) That oughta bring him back to his senses. Been flyin' so high he forgot what the earth feels like under him.

THISBE: (Sobering up) You're right, woman. Best we be gettin' home. You're right, like you *always* are, my wise owl.

(ARBYZENA, pleased, comes down the steps and helps remove the bits of snow from THISBE's clothes. ARMINTA is sitting on the porch steps.)

ARBYZENA: Glad you're comin' back to your senses, husband.

THADIUS: (Winking, to THISBE) My devil's brew has got itself a real whallop to it. Don't it, Thiz?

THISBE: (Taking ARBYZENA's hand in his) Not as much as my woman here, Thadius.

(THISBE and ARBYZENA EXIT toward S.L. wings walking hand-in-hand, as ARMINTA trails slowly after them, when she is stopped by THADIUS's words:)

THADIUS: Lucky man that takes Arminta Ogle for his woman.

ARMINTA: (Hurt) Too bad the only time you ain't mean is when you're dead drunk, Thadius Steed. Fate's withering away and you ain't doing nothing to help her. I'd rather sleep alone the rest of my days than be wedded to the likes of you.

(ARMINTA lingers at the marrying tree, touching it, wistfully for SEVERAL BEATS.)

ARBYZENA (OFF-STAGE): (Sharply) Arminta!

ARMINTA: (EXITING) Coming, Mother!

HOMER: (Confidentially, to THADIUS) There's one sad lass over-ripe for the pickin'.

(The front door opens, GRANNY, POLLY, and MANUEL ENTER the porch. HOMER rises from his rocking chair upon hearing GRANNY'S VOICE.)

GRANNY: (Calling to FATE inside the cabin) Take that medicine I give ya before you go to bed, child. (Closing the door, to THADIUS) Make sure she takes it, Thadius. She's awful weak. Go on in and give her a hand, now.

THADIUS: Nope. Fate can take care of herself. I gotta go see to my other milch cows in the barn. (EXITING to the barn.)

GRANNY: Can't you get through to him Homer? He's putting her under.

HOMER: I'm tryin' my darndest.

GRANNY: (To MANUEL) And you ain't helping her neither, Manuel. Her own papa disowning her!

MANUEL: (Searing look towards POLLY) She ain't no kin of mine.

GRANNY: (Anger mounting) Listen here, Manuel O'Dare! That newborn child in there is needin' herself a grand-daddy. You're the only one can be that for her. Just like you're the only daddy Fate's ever knowed.

MANUEL: Ain't no affair of nobody's.

GRANNY: I'm speakin' my mind, 'cause I got me a terrible foreboding. You both got yourselves a sweet little grandchild, now. You can't be wanting her world darkened by that ugly cloud of hatred you two been living under all these years. Tear down that barbed wire fence of deadly silence before it's too late! Do it for the child.

POLLY: I'm scared too, Granny. (To MANUEL) I'd be willing to take wire cutters to that fence of ours.

 MANUEL: . . .Tell my wife adultery's a sin *unforgivable* before the Lord.

HOMER: You be okay gettin' home, Louzilthy?

POLLY: Me 'n Manuel will be seein' her home, Uncle Homer. Button your coat, Granny. It's getting real cold. Don't you worry none, Uncle Homer.

HOMER: Appreciate it. (Kissing GRANNY's hand) Sleep tight, Louzilthy. (Teasing her) And don't be 'alettin' the bed bugs bite.

GRANNY: (Shoving him, playfully) Oh, get yourself to sleep, old man.

(HOMER begins to EXIT S.R. towards the barn, calling over his shoulder:)

HOMER: That I'll do, Louzilthy. Dreamin' all the while of your sunshine and soft hands. Dreamin' all the while of you.

(HOMER EXITS S.R. MANUEL is helping GRANNY down the porch steps and POLLY has walked ahead towards S.L. The MOON is casting a blue glow as though it were a finger pointing towards the Marrying Tree and the hewn tree-stump lectern. POLLY has stopped to look at it:)

POLLY: Why, look at that! It's as though the Good Lord's finger is pointing to our Marryin' Tree.

GRANNY: (Stops walking) Just a minute, Manuel.

(MANUEL stares at GRANNY, as the old woman's eyes shut tightly.)

MANUEL: You all right, Granny?

(GRANNY's eyes open as she looks from POLLY to MANUEL:)

GRANNY: Know what I just wished?

POLLY: What, Granny?

GRANNY: Wished you two would stop your unGodly silence before the Lord puts his hand on one of your shoulders and it's too late to bury your grudge. Fate's not happy. She's cravin' for the love she never got at home.

(MANUEL is looking up towards the sky.)

MANUEL: Looks like we're in for quite a storm.

(MANUEL, GRANNY, and POLLY EXIT S.L.
THE OWL HOOTS for several ominous beats.
FATE, in robe, ENTERS the porch from the cabin.
She is barefooted. Her hair is wild. Quietly, she
closes the front door behind her.   She hugs the porch
post, pressing her cheek to it, as she stares up towards
her mountain bald.)

FATE: (Looking out towards the mountain) Maybe
up there I'll find the peace I'm craving for. (FATE
moves towards S.L. where she is stopped by a
LIGHTNING FLASH followed by a DEAFENING
THUNDER CLAP. A BABY'S CRY IS HEARD
coming from inside the cabin.) Oh, baby! *Hope*, this
is the only thing your mama can do for you, now.
First was my mama's sin. Then, mine. And each day,
that shameful silence, killing a piece of us at a time.
I gotta try to break that sinful chain, so it won't hurt
you too, sweet angel. God bless!

(FATE runs off EXITING. BLACK OUT.)

SCENE TWO

> *It is later that same night. LIGHTNING*
> *FLASHES and THUNDER SOUNDS as*
> *FATE reaches the summit of the*
> *mountain bald. The APPALACHIAN*

HORNET'S frenzied WHIRRING
mirrors the frenzy of the storm.

FATE: (Shouting above the wind) Hate won't destroy your mama one silent year at a time, sweet darling. (Running her fingers through her hair) Hyram! Your hands are the wind pouring over me, now. Your lips are the raindrops on my cheeks. Your body is this mountain I love so underneath mine. Hyram don't leave me!

HYRAM (OFF-STAGE): (Voice echoing from the past) We are part of the divine scheme.

FATE: (Shocked) Hyram?

(OPENING HER ARMS, birdlike, FATE sways perilously close to the cliff's edge, fighting to hold her ground against the tug of the wind. LIGHTNING FLASHES and THUNDER PEALS.)

HYRAM (OFF-STAGE): (Echoing from the past) Death needs no apology here.

FATE: (To the heavens) Hyram! Let me soar to heaven with you!

(THE LIGHTS DIM as the WIND WAILS in ANGUISH. LIGHTNING FLASHES revealing the SWOOPING SHADOW OF A BIRD descending across the cyclorama from S.L. to

Steed's cabin S.R. THUNDER CRASHES.
BLACK OUT.)

SCENE THREE

*LIGHTS COME UP on the HEMLOCK
TREE weeping as rain drops through its
branches. The SOUND OF RAIN is
HEARD gently falling, as the LIGHTS
COME UP on Steed's homestead.
It is afternoon of the following day.
HOMER rocks solemnly in his
porch rocking chair.*

HOMER: One hell of a storm we had. (He
spits a wad of tobacco at the porch bell, making it
ring.) They're inside there, now. Layin' her out. So
she'll be fit to meet her Maker. I reckon she met Him
when He swept her clean off that mountain of hers
last night.

(THADIUS ENTERS the porch from the cabin. The
fire appears to have gone out of him. He sits slowly
on the top porch step.)

THADIUS: I can't stay inside this house no more.
(Remorsefully) I done it to her. Same as if I'd shot
her through the heart.

HOMER: Some things can't be stopped from
happening, Nephew. Fate wasn't right since the time
her baby come. Might've been a fever.

THADIUS: Nope. I done it. Cursing her every day.

HOMER: You had cause.

THADIUS. No, Uncle. In the middle of that storm last night, when I realized she was gone. . ..and Hyram's gone. . . .and even those good-for-nothin' Revenuers--*all* gone 'cause of me. Well, something changed inside of me.

HOMER: *Remorse.* It's good you're feelin' it. 'Cause sometimes I wondered if you was *human.*

THADIUS: I always thought feelings was just for womenfolk.

HOMER: Feelings ain't nothin' to be ashamed of.

THADIUS: I seen it too late.

HOMER: You still got plenty of living time ahead of you, Nephew

THADIUS: You know how much this place means to me, but I can't stay here no more.

HOMER: What're you sayin'?

THADIUS: I gotta leave the mountains for good.

HOMER: Punishing yourself ain't gonna make no difference--

THADIUS: I gotta go someplace where I can do some good without having to use a gun.

HOMER: And where would that place be?

THADIUS: Virginia. Them miners need somebody to help 'em get organized so they can have better working conditions--

(POLLY, who has been eavesdropping at the door, ENTERS the porch from the cabin, and sits on a chair beside HOMER. She stares blankly ahead:)

POLLY: And what about your *daughter*?

THADIUS: Polly, I don't know a lick about carin' for younguns Little girls need womenfolk to teach 'em things.

(MANUEL ENTERS from S.L. toting a shovel:)

MANUEL: It's dug, Thadius. Right up on that mountain bald, like you wanted.

THADIUS: Appreciate your taking care of that for me, Manuel.

MANUEL: Don't need no thanks. After all, Fate was *my* daughter.

THADIUS: Manuel, I got one more favor to ask of you.

MANUEL: Name it.

THADIUS: I'll be leavin' the mountains pretty soon. I need for you 'n Polly to take care of the child for me.

MANUEL: Leavin' the Smokies?

THADIUS: You're the child's grandparents. It seems fittin' fer you to be doin' the raising.

POLLY: (To MANUEL) This would be a chance for us to start anew, Manuel. Haven't we caused enough hurt with our feuding? We could give Hope the proper family love her mama never knowed.

MANUEL: (With difficulty) All right, Polly. We can try.

(POLLY'S hand covers MANUEL'S.)

THADIUS: Good. 'Cause tryin's the best any of us can do. Ain't that right, Uncle Homer?

HOMER: Yup.

(BLACK OUT.)

EPILOGUE

LIGHTS COME UP the following morning at FATE'S gravesite where the MOUNTAIN FOLK have assembled and FOBIDIAH'S FUNERAL SERMON is concluding:

105

FOBIDIAH: (Finishing his sermon) Remember friends, endings are also beginnings.

POLLY: (Looking at MANUEL) Amen, Lord.

FOBIDIAH: Before we end our funeral meeting, I'd like y'all to see the words writ on this here tombstone. (Removes the tarp from the headstone) Words written by Thadius Steed. A man who'll be *exiling* himself from these mountains he loves, so *he* can begin anew.

GRANNY: *Begin anew.*

GROUP: Amen.

HOMER: Thadius, read us them words you writ.

THADIUS: Fate O'Dare Steed, 1894 to 1911
Budded on Earth
To Bloom in Heaven.

 (THADIUS places flowers on FATE'S grave.
The OGLES AND OWNBYS pass by the gravesite,
 paying their respects, EXITING.

UNCLE HOMER and GRANNY stop before EXITING.)

GRANNY: Lord go with thee, Thadius Steed.

(HOMER bear hugs THADIUS.)

HOMER: We'll all be thinking on you, Nephew.

THADIUS: Be thinking on you too, you ornery old bar.

(HOMER and GRANNY EXIT with FOBIDIAH. THADIUS remains at the gravesite for several beats. He turns to look out at the Smokies.)

ORVAL (OFF-STAGE):   (Echoing from the past) Must be some sight those Smoky Mountains of yours.

THADIUS: Best sight the Lord could ever give us mortals. Makes a man feel Godlike just being here. Seeing how we mortals can help to make this earth of ours a hell. . .or a *heaven*.

(THADIUS EXITS into the theater house as "*SOMETIMES*" reprises:)
ENSEMBLE: (SINGING)
SOMETIMES WORK, SOMETIMES PLAY
MAN AND WOMAN GO ON YOUR WAY
BLESS THE NIGHT AND HOPE EACH DAY
SOMETIMES GOOD, SOMETIMES

SOMETIMES SUN, SOMETIMES STORM
A LITTLE TIME AND LOVIN'S BORN
FIND THE ROSE, FORGET THE THORN
*SOMETIMES GOOD, SOMETIMES**
END OF PLAY.
*Music for "SOMETIMES" hymn by Barbara Rottman available upon request.

ABOUT THE PLAY & THE PLAYWRIGHT

LORD OF THE SMOKIES was initially presented as the musical *THADIUS STEED* with music by BARBARA ROTTMAN and lyrics by Lichtman/Rottman. Its first staged reading at U.S.C.'s Stop Gap Theatre featured BORIS APLON, JAVIER GRAJEDA, MYLA, DEBRA MORENO, STEVE CUDEN, DONNA SZOLLOSSI, JACKIE TRUDEAU, PATTY LOEB, and CHRIS SAMPSON. The musical's second staged reading at Beverly Hills' Theatre 40 featured: ROD LOOMIS, KIM CONRAD, WALTER ATAMANLUK, HORST EHRHARDT, SANDRA LAMONT, and EDITH FIELDS.

LORD OF THE SMOKIES was the inaugural play of The Norris Theater's New Play Discovery Series [see review that follows]. The cast featured: MICHAEL PUTNAM, LINDA PUTNAM, BILLY CREAMER, STEPHEN WAYNE-FISHER, LLOYD HESLIP, FRANCES ROTH, BOB MCCAMAN, RITA WILLENS, PATRICIA HIGGINS, NANCY CAMPBELL, SUSAN SACHS, WARREN KAPLAN, and STEVE CUDEN. Musical direction by LESLIE BACK.

The play was a FINALIST for THE SERGEL DRAMA PRIZE and also THE CRAIG PLAYWRITING CONTEST.

Myla Lichtman-Fields' plays have received awards and have been produced throughout the U.S. As a staff writer at Universal Studios, she penned TV episodics, MOWs, and an NBC Special. She has a Ph.D. in Communications/Drama with a minor in Film from U.S.C. Myla is a member of The Dramatists Guild, The Writers Guild, and PEN.

PALOS VERDES PENINSULA NEWS   Saturday, February 18, 1984   5

'Smokies' Smolders With a Fulfilled Dramatic Promise

By RICHARD ESPOSITO
News Arts Editor

The inaugural work of the North Community Theater's New Play Discovery Series provided both a noteworthy reading of a classic tale and an opportunity for the community to support one of its own.

That opportunity was not wasted Thursday night, when a nearly full house gave an enthusiastic reception to Myla Lichtman-Fields' Appalachian tragedy "Lord of the Smokies." As promised, the staged reading of Lichtman-Fields' play showed many of the possibilities and much of the potential woven into the work.

Following a long time interest in stage Appalachian culture, Lichtman-Fields even traveled to Tennessee's Great Smoky Mountains to absorb the accents and flavors of the region. The care of authenticity that results from her research proves that the materials there have not yet been mined of all their dramatic potential.

Inspired by the simultaneously tumultuous and God-fearing toil folk, Appalachian seems, in fact, to be the perfect setting for a new look at Euripides' tragedy of Hippolytus. Minded

of the gods and doomed by fate, the Smoky Mountain's hillbillies are America's ancient Greeks, and true to the play's classic roots, they are driven by passion to their ultimate undoing.

Written in three acts, "Lord of the Smokies" was presented in two halves Thursday night, with an intermission bisecting Act Two. The first half unfolded with a steady momentum that seemed overfused a bit in part two. This should, however, be overcome easily once the work is fully staged at the hands of a director who can help sustain the pace and strengthen a few of the peripheral characters.

Overall, the reading did justice to the author's research and gave ample evidence of the dramatist's skill. The following Michael Putnam as Theldeus Sired Chesney, Linda Putnam as his niece with Pam O'Hare (Phaedra) and Warren Kaplan as Taadeaus' brother Hyram (Hippolytus) were compelling as the lead trio. With actors such as these, as well as the unrehearsed Bob McCarren and the sage Billy Creamer in a fully staged production, "Lord of the Smokies" would indeed be something in which the author and her community could take pride.

"The nearly full house gave an enthusiastic reception to Myla Lichtman-Fields' Appalachian tragedy *Lord of the Smokies*. A fully staged production would indeed be something in which the author and her community could take pride."

111

Myla Lichtman-Fields' plays available thru **Lulu.com**:

4 MUSICMAKERS PLAYS:
FELIX & FANNY
VS. ROBERT SCHUMANN
SERENADE
CLARA & JOHANNES

IRISH PLAY TRILOGY:
BRIGID OF KILDARE
AN IRISH SONATA
THE STONE OF KILHARA

AMERICANA PLAYS:
SATAN AMONGST US
SPIRITS OF THE OLD MANSE
THE PEACEMAKERS
LORD OF THE SMOKIES
THE WETBACK
LEARNING TO DANCE IN THE RAIN

FANTASY PLAYS:
THE SCANDALMAKERS (About Mary Shelley)
WAGADU (An African Mythodrama)
FAUSTINE (A Female Faust)

www.ingramcontent.com/pod-product-compliance
Lightning Source LLC
Chambersburg PA
CBHW030344290526
45785CB00004B/1591